YOU
MLA
NA

The FRUIT of the VINE

To my friend Dr. Young
"As iron sharpeneth iron"

The FRUIT of the VINE

The Scriptural Case For Temperance

By
Louis F. DeBoer

Copyright © 2000 Louis F. DeBoer
All Rights Reserved

No part of this book may be reproduced in any form, or by any electronic or mechanical means, without permission in writing from the author, except by a reviewer who may quote brief passages in a review, and by writers who wish to quote brief passages in their work.

Cover Illustration: Canaan, the land of promise was a fruitful land and this fertility was especially manifested in the abundance of the fruit of the vine.

Published by:
The American Presbyterian Press
1459 Boston Neck Road
Saunderstown, RI 02874
www.amprpress.com

ISBN 0-9703712-2-5

Printed in the United States by
Morris Publishing
3212 E. Hwy 30
Kearney, NE 68847
1-800-650-7888

Table of Contents

ACKNOWLEDGEMENTS

I want to express my appreciation to Dr. Stephen Reynolds of the L. L. Reynolds Foundation for his assistance in bringing this book to publication. It is through a grant from the Foundation that the means have been made available for publishing this work. Dr. Reynolds' personal commitment to a full and scriptural defense of the doctrine of temperance and the generosity of the Foundation are a real encouragement to me to persevere in a cause that will be resisted by many and scorned by not a few.

I also want to acknowledge the assistance of Rev. Allan Wagner, who initially gave me a photocopy of Ritchie's book, *Scripture Testimony Against Intoxicating Wine* and to Dr. Charles Butler, who gave me a copy of Dr. Reynolds' book, *The Biblical Approach to Alcohol*. I profited not only by a study of these books, but also by our discussions of this issue. Additionally, I want to thank my son Louis Elijah who assists with the proofreading of each manuscript, and my wife Faith, whose artistic talents are the final court of appeal for any issues with the cover artwork.

However, ultimately our thanks must be to a gracious providence that has enabled this project to come to fruition, and to the Holy Spirit, who inspired the Scriptures that are the foundation on which all this is built. May the Lord be pleased to use this work to his honor and glory, and in the defense of the faith, and to the instruction of his elect in sanctification.

FOREWORD

The thesis of this book, that the Scriptures teach abstinence from alcoholic beverages, is not original. Neither is the approach to defending that doctrine original, although to many it may appear to be so. This is because historically the temperance movement has not enjoyed a full and adequate scriptural defense of its position. All that is original with this work is in the details. The exact arguments and the specific texts cited to prove each point may be mine, but the overall thrust of this book is borrowed from others who have gone before. I would like to cite at least three from whose writings I have profited. I will state them in the order that I discovered them, read them, and was influenced by them. The first one is *Bible Wines or the Laws of Fermentation* by William Patton. It was originally published some time in the last century. My copy is a reprint from the Challenge Press, which issued it sometime back in the 1970's. Since they did not print the original title page, I can only guess as to its origin. However, since the latest quotations that it makes from periodicals of the time are from the 1870's, I presume that it was likely published shortly thereafter. It not only makes many of the pertinent scriptural arguments, and establishes the generic nature of some of the scriptural words for wine, but it gives a detailed analysis of the science of fermentation as it was understood at that time, with the object of showing how the new wine was preserved and kept from fermentation in Biblical times.

The next book worthy of mention is *Scripture Testimony Against Intoxicating Wine* by the Rev. William Ritchie of Scotland, and his work was published in 1866. I have a photocopy of his book. This work is the most exhaustive in its review of the scriptural words for, and the scriptural references to wine. His thoroughness makes this book especially valuable and one of the better works on the subject. Finally, there is a contemporary book that is still in print. I refer to Dr. Stephen Reynolds' work entitled, *The Biblical Approach to Alcohol*. Dr. Reynolds' work is very scholarly and its value lies especially in his abilities in the field of linguistics and his knowledge of the original languages of Scripture.

All three of these books are worthy of being read by any serious student of this issue. The present work is not offered to compete with these original works. Rather it is written in recognition of the fact that at least two of the three are out of print. It was also written to provide a more simple, direct, less exhaustive, and less scholarly, presentation of these important truths. As such I hope it will be well received by the reader.

Saunderstown, Rhode Island

January 10, 2000

CHAPTER 1
INTRODUCTION

The question of the use of alcoholic beverages has been an issue in the church of Jesus Christ for centuries. It has not, as with respect to some other doctrinal issues, been a matter of conflict between professing Christians who accept the Scriptures as an exclusive and infallible guide in these matters, and those who have a more liberal construction of things. Rather it has been an issue that has divided conservative Christians who are committed to the inspiration, inerrancy, and sufficiency of Scripture. The issue is therefore not allegiance to Scripture, but rather the understanding of Scripture. And the reason for this is that the Scriptures themselves appear to give an "*uncertain sound*" on this matter.

There is a real tension between texts on the subject of alcohol and wine as they are presented in the English translations of the Bible. The Scriptures often appear to both unilaterally praise and unilaterally condemn that object which is called wine. The following texts will make this abundantly clear. First we have a series of texts that praise wine and regard it as the bounty and the blessing of a gracious God.

And thou shalt bestow that money for whatsoever thy soul lusteth after, for oxen, or for sheep, or for wine, or for strong drink, or for whatsoever thy soul desireth: and thou shalt eat there before the LORD thy God, and thou shalt rejoice, thou, and thine household. Deuteronomy 14:26

The Fruit of the Vine

Israel then shall dwell in safety alone: the fountain of Jacob shall be upon a land of corn and wine; also his heavens shall drop down dew. Deuteronomy 33:28

He causeth the grass to grow for the cattle, and herb for the service of man: that he may bring forth food out of the earth; And wine that maketh glad the heart of man, and oil to make his face to shine, and bread which strengtheneth man's heart. Psalm 104:14-15

For how great is his goodness, and how great is his beauty! corn shall make the young men cheerful, and new wine the maids. Zechariah 9:17

And they of Ephraim shall be like a mighty man, and their heart shall rejoice as through wine: yea, their children shall see it, and be glad; their heart shall rejoice in the LORD. Zechariah 10:7

These texts all set forth wine as a blessing of God and as something to be enjoyed. However, then we also have a series of texts that set forth wine as a curse and something to be avoided.

Wine is a mocker, strong drink is raging: and whosoever is deceived thereby is not wise. Proverbs 20:1

Who hath woe? who hath sorrow? who hath contentions? who hath babbling? who hath wounds without cause? who hath redness of eyes? They that tarry long at the wine; they that go to seek mixed wine. Look not thou upon the wine when it is red, when it giveth his colour in the cup, when it moveth itself aright. At the last it biteth like a serpent, and stingeth like an adder. Proverbs 23:29-32

It is not for kings, O Lemuel, it is not for kings to drink wine; nor for princes strong drink: Lest they drink, and forget the law, and pervert the judgment of any of the afflicted. Proverbs 31:4-5

Whoredom and wine and new wine take away the heart. Hosea 4:11

MODERATION:

Historically there has had to be some way of resolving the tension produced by these seemingly irreconcilable texts. Traditionally this has been done by postulating that those verses that praise wine have its moderate use in view, while those that condemn it have its excessive use, that is its abuse, in view. However, that is a very unsatisfactory solution. One really needs to strain these texts to force that interpretation on them consistently. The texts that praise wine do so unreservedly, with no warnings about the potentially disastrous results of immoderate use. Similarly, the texts that condemn wine do so in such explicit terms, that it is hard to imagine that the object of such condemnations and of such warnings is legitimate when used in moderation. This is especially true when the latter object is something that we are to guard against, as it will deceive its users. It is an object that we are not even to look at in a way of coveting or desiring it, because the end result of coveting this object is to be stung with its poison, as by a deadly, venomous snake. Kings especially are not warned to be moderate in its use, but to absolutely forsake the use of this particular beverage. And logically speaking, it does not compute that the limitation of moderate use can justify sanctioning something so explicitly condemned.

TEMPERANCE MOVEMENTS:

Due to the difficulty of reconciling these texts and due to the preponderant weight of opinion that some texts clearly do approve of wine, much of the debate has historically taken place on practical rather than on scriptural grounds. The temperance movements of the nineteenth century were chiefly driven by professing Christians of various denominations. And the arguments that fueled the debate for temperance, or abstinence with respect to alcoholic beverages, were to quote the Scriptures condemning wine and to set forth in horrific detail the practical evils resulting from alcohol abuse. They trained the guns of the debate on the irrefutable evils of alcoholism among the urban proletariat of America's cities, and on the equally devastating horrors of the saloon traffic, with its attendant prostitution and gambling, on the western frontier. They documented the high social cost of the abuse of alcohol, the vice, the broken homes, the poverty, etc., that attended its general use. And they were so effective that they succeeded in legislating the ban of its manufacture, sale, and consumption in this nation through the XVIII Amendment of the Constitution in 1919. But it was a Pyrrhic victory because they had given up the high ground. All the practical proclamations against the evils of alcoholism could not in themselves resolve the apparent tension of the scriptural testimony. And neither could it provide an irrefutable argument against those texts that appeared to sanction the use of alcoholic wine. Therefore the proponents of the Reformation principle, "*Sola scriptura,*" those who held to the principle that the Bible is the only rule of faith and practice, held the ideological high ground. And their interpretations of Scripture vindicated the moderate use of alcoholic wine.

Fortunately, there was a minority of Christian advocates of temperance who were prepared to argue the issue strictly on scriptural grounds. Unfortunately, they were in the minority and their expositions of Scripture did not dominate the debate over temperance. Fortunately, some of their writings have survived and come down to us. Unfortunately, these writings have been, for the most part, long out of print. However, a study of these writings reveals a new and far superior way of reconciling the apparent contradictions in the scriptural witness with respect to wine in the English Bible. It is to resurrect their scriptural arguments in a simple and concise form, and to present them to the Christian public, that this book is being written.

These writings basically set forth a new paradigm of interpreting the texts that deal with wine. The authors all did what one must do when there is an apparent difficulty in the translation from which one is working. One must go back to the Hebrew and the Greek Scriptures, the original inerrant, inspired Scriptures, and seek to resolve the issue there. After all, it is only the Holy Spirit speaking in Scripture that is our ultimate standard of truth, and not any translation. One of the weaknesses of many translations, including the Authorized Version, which was the one in use during the temperance debates, is that distinctions in the original text, such as different Hebrew or Greek words used by the Holy Spirit, are eliminated as they are frequently translated by the same English word. This was partly the case with wine in our translation. These particular authors went back to the Scriptures and did in-depth studies on the Hebrew and Greek words that were translated as wine or its cognates.

The result of these studies was the conclusion that some of the key Greek and Hebrew words* translated as wine are used generically. That is, they are words that stand for wine in the generic sense. They are used to represent wine per se, whether it be fermented wine or new wine, whether it be alcoholic wine or grape juice. One must therefore determine from the context, if possible, which type of wine

---

* There are a total of eight Hebrew words and two Greek words that are rendered in the English Bible by the word "wine" or "strong drink." Some of these are used in a generic sense and some have specific reference to a particular type of wine. Some words are used repeatedly throughout the Hebrew or Greek Scriptures and some are used only in a few instances. This study has concentrated on the dominant words that are used in the key texts on the question of temperance.

is being referred to. One needs to understand that the Hebrews, although obviously familiar with the practical results of the fermentation of grape juice, had no real scientific understanding of that process. Therefore they had no word for alcohol. It was not possible, and neither should we expect, for them to use modern terms such as alcoholic wine based on our scientific understanding of the distinction between fermented and unfermented wines. They therefore sometimes used the same word for all beverages that came from the grape, the fruit of the vine, and only from the context, or by use of additional adjectives, could the distinction as to the type of wine be brought out. In the Scriptures wine is wine, a beverage made from the blood of the grape. It can be new wine, that is "must,"* or grape juice. It can be fermented wine. They are both included in the generic word translated as wine.

This, as one can readily grasp, is another way of resolving the dilemma that readers of the English Bible have had regarding its testimony with respect to wine. This can simply and clearly explain for us why what appears to be the same object is both praised as a providential blessing of a gracious God and also likened to the venom of deadly reptiles. As the scriptural words stand for two radically different types of wine it is eminently logical that the Scriptures should also have radically different testimonies with respect to them. We will begin to review these word studies and show from the Scriptures that this understanding of the Biblical testimony concerning wine is the correct one.

---

* "Must" is an Old English word for grape juice or new wine. It comes from *vinum mustum*, Latin for new wine.

CHAPTER 2
YAYIN
יַיִן

Of all the words used in the Greek and Hebrew Scriptures that are translated as wine this is the most important one. Not only does it occur 141 times in the Hebrew Bible, but the Septuagint* translators translated it as *oinos* (οἶνος), which is almost exclusively the word used in the Greek New Testament for wine. Therefore a study of the word "*yayin*" will not only reveal what the Israelites meant when they spoke of wine, but will also serve as a foundation for interpreting what the New Testament authors said on the subject of wine. It is thus a crucial word study for the issue of temperance.

It is important to establish the terms of the debate at this point. The position that we are contesting is known as the "one wine" position. It says that wine, is wine, is wine, and that wine is an alcoholic beverage. The position that we are advocating is the "two wines" position. This says that wine may be wine, but that there are at least two different kinds of wine. It says that there is new wine in an unfermented state and that there is alcoholic wine in a fermented state. It is our purpose to show that, at least in the scriptural terminology, that the "one wine" theory is wrong and that *yayin* refers to both fermented and unfermented wine. That it refers to fermented wine is agreed to by all and therefore

---

* The Septuagint was a widely used translation of the Old Testament into Greek for use by the Greek speaking Jews of the dispersion. It was tranlsated during the intertestamental period in Alexandria, Egypt by a group of seventy Jewish scholars, hence its name which means seventy.

that point is not at issue. All that we need to do is show at least one verse that uses *yayin* to clearly refer to unfermented wine. If we can do that we have established our position. We intend to do better than that, as there are a number of texts that will support our position. Once the two wine position has been established then we can proceed to examine the contexts, determine if possible the nature of the wine being referred to, and begin to draw the appropriate conclusions. In that way we plan to definitely establish the scriptural case for temperance. It is our contention that once the "two wine" position has been established, the entire position of the moderate use of alcoholic wine begins to crumble. This is because the defenders of moderate use constantly appeal to the texts that approve of new wine to justify their consumption of fermented wine. Once that crutch is taken away their position cannot stand.

Before we begin our study I would like to say a few words about semantics. Since we are contesting the traditional and historic understanding of these texts we have a difficult enough task before us. I do not wish to compound this difficulty by getting embroiled in issues of semantics. Due to the contemporary use of the word "wine" to refer exclusively to fermented wine some may find the idea of "two wines" preposterous. To them wine is wine and the unferemented blood of the grape is not wine but merely grape juice. In other words they have a semantic prejudice against the two wines argument. To accommodate their prejudices I should phrase the debate in terms of wine (i.e., alcoholic wine, the only kind of wine they acknowledge) and grape juice. This is certainly a viable way of proceeding. However there is probably just as much semantic prejudice against translating Greek and Hebrew words, that have been translated as wine from time immemorial, by the new term, grape juice. I have chosen to do the former rather than the latter and to refer to two different kinds of wine. There are two reasons for this. First of all, as Patten has documented in his book *Bible Wines*, there is historic precedent in both the English language and in other European languages for using wine in a generic sense to refer to both fermented and non-fermented beverages made from grapes. And secondly, and most importantly, the Scriptures themselves adopt this mode of speaking. The Scriptures, with only rare exceptions, use the same word for both alcoholic wine and grape juice. The Holy Spirit has adopted this mode of speaking in the Scriptures and that is the mode that we will employ. From the Old Testament Hebrews to the members of the New Testament Church, the people of God have been used to having all the beverages of the grape, whether fermented or not, defined by the same generic words. And we plan to continue that manner of speaking. Now let us proceed to establish from Scripture that that is indeed the case.

We have already noted that the issue of whether *yayin* ever refers to fermented wine is not in debate. The following texts make that abundantly clear.

And he drank of the ***wine,**** *and was drunken; and he was uncovered within his tent...And Noah awoke from his* ***wine,*** *and knew what his younger son had done unto him.* Genesis 9:21,24

And Eli said unto her, How long wilt thou be drunken? put away thy ***wine*** *from thee. And Hannah answered and said, No, my lord, I am a woman of a sorrowful spirit: I have drunk neither* ***wine*** *nor strong drink, but have poured out my soul before the LORD.* 1 Samuel 1:14-15

It is not for kings, O Lemuel, it is not for kings to drink ***wine;*** *nor for princes strong drink: Lest they drink, and*

---

* In each chapter, in the Scripture quotations, I have highlighted with bold print the translation of the Greek or Hebrew word that is under consideration.

forget the law, and pervert the judgment of any of the afflicted. Proverbs 31:4-5

Woe unto them that rise up early in the morning, that they may follow strong drink; that continue until night, till ***wine*** *inflame them!* Isaiah 5:11

Since in all of the above texts (and there are many more) the consequences of drinking *yayin* is intoxication, it is clear that in these passages the word must refer to fermented wine. We can now proceed to examine the texts that use *yayin* in a context that definitively establishes that it is referring to new wine, to the juice expressed from the fruit of the vine. The clearest text for our purpose reads as follows…

And gladness is taken away, and joy out of the plentiful field; and in the vineyards there shall be no singing, neither shall there be shouting: the treaders shall tread out no ***wine*** *in their presses; I have made their vintage shouting to cease.* Isaiah 16:10

Now it is obvious to all, that what is treaded out in the winepress cannot be fermented wine, but has to be new wine. This solitary text has already established our position, but there are more.

Binding his foal unto the vine, and his ass's colt unto the choice vine; he washed his garments in ***wine****, and his clothes in the blood of grapes.* Genesis 49:11

Now since his garments are the same as his clothes it naturally also follows that *yayin* is the "*blood of grapes*", that is it is new wine from the winevat, pressed out from the grapes.

He shall separate himself from ***wine*** *and strong drink, and shall drink no vinegar of* ***wine****, or vinegar of strong drink, neither shall he drink any liquor of grapes, nor eat moist grapes, or dried. All the days of his separation shall he eat* *nothing that is made of the vine tree, from the kernels even to the husk.* Numbers 6:3-4

This is a particularly interesting text for our purposes. The word for liquor is "*mishrah*" (מִשְׁרָה) and means maceration, or steeping in a liquid. It refers to the practice of taking the residue of pressed grapes from the winepress and steeping them in water to produce a kind of weak grape juice. The point of the text is that the Nazarite is forbidden to eat or drink anything that has come from the vine. This prohibition includes fresh grapes as well as raisins or dried grapes, and includes the steepings of the residue in the winepress, as well as vinegar made from wine. It certainly has to include fresh grape juice and fermented wine as well, as these are also produced from the vine. However there is only one word used to express both, and that word is "*yayin.*" (We will establish in a later chapter that the word for strong drink does not have reference to anything produced from the vine. However if anyone disputes that, and seeks to maintain that strong drink has reference to alcoholic wine made from grape juice, then *yayin* definitely has to mean grape juice in this passage and our position is still established.) *Yayin* therefore has to mean both new and fermented wine and therefore perfectly establishes our position.

I said in mine heart, Go to now, I will prove thee with mirth, therefore enjoy pleasure: and, behold, this also is vanity. I said of laughter, It is mad: and of mirth, What doeth it? I sought in mine heart to give myself unto ***wine****, yet acquainting mine heart with wisdom; and to lay hold on folly, till I might see what was that good for the sons of men, which they should do under the heaven all the days of their life.* Ecclesiastes 2:1-3

In this passage Solomon is establishing the vanity of the pleasures of this life. As he experimentally tested the pleasures of this life and by the standard of wisdom found them all wanting, and but exercises in vanity, he includes wine. To which kind of wine was he referring? It is hard to believe that Solomon made a conscious decision to give himself to alcoholic wine, to become as it were an alcoholic. In fact the wisdom of which he himself wrote under inspiration in the Proverbs, forbade kings to drink intoxicating wine (See Proverbs 31:4-5 quoted above). It is only reasonable to conclude that he decided to try out the good life and live luxuriously with the finest cuisine and not that he made a decision to test out the dubious pleasures of intoxication and drunkeness. We could seek to multiply such references but the above should be more than sufficient to convince any impartial reader that *yayin* can and does sometimes refer to unfermented, non-alcoholic wine.

If this dual meaning of *yayin* as wine seems confusing, it is not less so than the etymology of the word itself. Strong has it as derived from a root meaning "to effervesce," and therefore as referring to fermented wine.* Young relates it to a root meaning of "pressed out," and as referring to grape juice. It is our contention that, whatever its etymology, it came to refer to both, and must be regarded as a generic term.

Having established that *yayin* can refer to two sorts of wine, we now proceed to an examination of what the Scriptures say with respect to *yayin*. As previously stated the word "*yayin*" occurs 141 times in the Hebrew Scriptures. Of these it occurs a total of 33 times in a neutral sense without any hint of either approval or condemnation. It is also used a total of 24 times in a context where it is regarded with a sense of approval. And then finally it is

---

* This does not necessarily require one to assume that it refers to alcoholic wine and that the effervescence is that of fermentation. As the grape juice is expressed from the grapes in the winepress it is known to foam. This foaming could be the effervescence being noted.

used 71 times when it is accompanied by warnings against it, warnings consisting both of specific admonitions against its use, as well as warnings of its destructive power by example.

Since there are a total of 141 instances of *yayin* we can not examine all the texts where it appears, as we will of some other words in our study. We can start by omitting the 33 instances where it is cited in a neutral context, as we will glean little that is definitive from such texts. Then we will examine representative texts from those that approve of *yayin* and those that condemn it. We will seek to establish two points. First, that the inconsistency of these texts prove that they are not referring to the same thing. Secondly, that those texts that condemn alcoholic *yayin* cannot be interpreted in a way that the condemnation is pointed only at its abuse and not at the article itself. Let us proceed to demonstrate the first point, starting with the following texts.

In the day of our king the princes have made him sick with bottles of ***wine****; he stretched out his hand with scorners.* Hosea 7:5

In this passage the word for bottles is "*chemath.*" The translators of the Authorized Version took this as derived from *chemeth* (חֵמֶת), which means a small skin bottle or wineskin. But more modern scholarship is agreed that it is properly derived from *chemah* (חֵמָה), which can mean heat, fury, or poison.* Six times it is translated in the Hebrew Scriptures as poison. In this context we have to ask what made the king sick, the heat of the wine, the anger of the wine, or the poison of the wine? The answer is obvious, only poison, not heat or anger, can and does inevitably make one sick. It is a common fallacy that alcoholic beverages, particularly potent liquors, make one warm. It is thought

---

* See Stephen J. Reynolds, *The Biblical Approach to Alcohol*, Princeton University Press, pp. 63-66.

that a nip of brandy, or a shot of whiskey, or a cup of rum, etc., will keep one warm in the cold. However it is the unanimous testimony of scientists and medical people that it is counterproductive to attempt to keep warm by drinking alcohol. Therefore there is no scientific or medical basis for the supposition that the heat of too much wine made the king sick. It is important to note that the text speaks of the poison of wine, and not of the poison in the wine. If the latter, it could be argued that poisonous, or drugged wine, was given to the king. The text does not allow for that interpretation and speaks of the poison of wine, the poison that inherently exists in all wine, in all fermented wine that is. This interpretation is supported by the use of *chemah* in the following text…

*Their **wine** is the **poison** of dragons, and the cruel venom of asps.* Deuteronomy 32:33

And we have already examined the following text, which completes the trilogy of texts that refer to wine as poison.

*Look not thou upon the **wine** when it is red, when it giveth his colour in the cup, when it moveth itself aright. At the last it biteth like a serpent, and stingeth like an adder.* Proverbs 23:31-32

The word "poison" may not be here but the inference remains clear. The poison of the wine will inevitably strike those who are given to it, and the results will be like the bite of venomous, poisonous snakes.

Now, our question is, "Are these texts consistent with those that speak of wine as an innocent blessing of God provided in his gracious providence for his people?" In short, are the above texts consistent with the following texts? Do they all relate to exactly the same article of food, do they refer to the exact same beverage?

He causeth the grass to grow for the cattle, and herb for the service of man: that he may bring forth food out of the earth; And ***wine*** *that maketh glad the heart of man, and oil to make his face to shine, and bread which strengtheneth man's heart.* Psalm 104:14-15

And thou shalt bestow that money for whatsoever thy soul lusteth after, for oxen, or for sheep, or for ***wine****, or for strong drink, or for whatsoever thy soul desireth: and thou shalt eat there before the LORD thy God, and thou shalt rejoice, thou, and thine household.* Deuteronomy 14:26

And they of Ephraim shall be like a mighty man, and their heart shall rejoice as through ***wine****: yea, their children shall see it, and be glad; their heart shall rejoice in the LORD.* Zechariah 10:7

Now, we are compelled to ask, does God make man's heart happy by his gracious providence and the bounty of his creation, or by the chemical action of alcohol on the brain? Are worshippers rejoicing before the Lord commanded to lust after alcohol? Do these texts, yea, can these texts, really refer to the same thing that is condemned as akin to the venom of reptiles? We think not and neither does the Apostle Paul who teaches…

"*Nevertheless he left not himself without witness, in that he did good, and gave us rain from heaven, and fruitful seasons, filling our hearts with food and gladness*" Acts 14:17.

According to Paul it is God's gracious providence in the form of bountiful harvests that brings gladness and that is how we ought to interpret the above noted texts from the Hebrew Scriptures.

And even for those who would disagree with us, we must pass on to our second point. Do these condemnations of wine condemn wine in itself or only its excessive use? Do these texts say that the poison consists of excess of wine? Do they say that the immoderation is the poison? The answer is clearly no. It is the poison of the wine itself that makes one sick. It is the wine itself that is likened to the "*poison of dragons, and the cruel venom of asps.*" It is true that Proverbs 23:30 speaks of those who linger long with their wine, inferring excessive use and abuse. However, in the very next verse it states that we are not even to look on alcoholic wine with desire, to lust after it. And it is the consequence of breaking that admonition, that we are warned, will result in consequences akin to the bite of venomous reptiles.

So far we have said little about the warnings against alcoholic wine by example, but a few words on that subject are in order. As we have already noted there are a total of 71 texts that refer to *yayin* in a context of warning. This constitutes an overwhelming testimony in Scripture on the dangers of *yayin*. Let us examine some of these examples. The very first mention in the Scriptures of *yayin* is Genesis 9, where we have the sad tale of Noah's drunkeness. The consequences of this folly on the patriarch's part were shame, nakedness, and the entailing of a curse on the posterity of one of his sons. This is the very first mention of wine in the Bible and the very first sin noted after the great flood. After many years of faithful service, of steadfast testimony to God's truth, we see Noah brought to shame by alcoholic wine. This is the only sin recorded in the Scriptures concerning Noah, and it was occasioned by alcohol. After God's great and fearsome judgments on the generation of the flood and their sin, after they were all swept away and the earth had, as it were, a new beginning with a faithful remnant, it was alcohol that occasioned a new fall into sin. Is there not a great and terrible warning here against that which can be so destructive in its effects? Is it not truly well described as a poison! Are we not hereby taught to shun such dangers attended with such consequences? And the very next usage of *yayin* in Genesis 14 presents a totally different picture. Here we have a blessed event. Here we see Abraham returning victoriously from the rescue of Lot and the slaughter of the kings. Here we see him met by Melchisedek, king of peace, priest of the Most High God, and a type of Christ. Here we see him refreshed with gifts of food, with bread and wine. Are we to actually believe that this is the same wine that is compared to the venom of snakes? Are we to believe this is the same wine that had such dire consequences in the life of Noah? Must not *yayin* then refer to two different sorts of wine? And if we turn the page again we again find ourselves at the opposite extreme of the Scripture's testimony concerning wine. In Genesis 19 we have another example of the disastrous results of the use of alcoholic wine. We see the daughters of Lot, raised up in the ways of Sodom, conspire to make their father drunk with wine, and to commit acts of incest so as to perpetuate their Father's seed. We note the evil results in the history of Israel and the generations of enmity between Israel and Ammon and Moab, the endless conflict, battles, oppressions, and misery, all entailed by the corrupting consequences of using alcoholic wine. And again the next use of *yayin* is a total change of scene. Here, in Genesis 49, we have a prophetic reference to the coming Messiah, to Jesus the Christ, washing his garments in the "*blood of grapes.*" Do not these alternating testimonies in the very first book of the Bible, set the tone for our attitude to wine? Do they not compel us to believe that there have to be two different kinds of wine that are being spoken of? Do they not teach us by precept and example which kind of wine we are to rejoice with, and which kind of wine we are to avoid as a hiker would avoid rattlesnakes?

We have not yet exhausted the testimony of God's word with respect to *yayin*. But I believe that we have by now said enough. For those who are convinced of the inerrancy of Scripture, for whom even a single scriptural witness is enough, surely the above documentation ought to be sufficient. We still have much more to say, and other inspired words to study, and other incidents to examine. But by now, I pray that every reader will have been convinced that there are two kinds of wine and two radically different bodies of testimony regarding them. Let us now proceed to build on that foundation.

CHAPTER 3
TIROSH
תִּירשׁ תִּירוֹשׁ

The word "*tirosh*" occurs 38 times in the Hebrew Scriptures. Of these 38 citations, 37 of them refer to it as a blessing promised by, or provided by, a gracious God for his children. Only once it is rendered in a context where it is condemned as something that men are abusing. We will deal with this lone text separately further on. A sampling of the typical texts, showing the beneficent nature of *tirosh* as a blessing of God, is as follows…

Therefore God give thee of the dew of heaven, and the fatness of the earth, and plenty of corn and ***wine****.* Genesis 27:28

And he will love thee, and bless thee, and multiply thee: he will also bless the fruit of thy womb, and the fruit of thy land, thy corn, and thy ***wine****, and thine oil, the increase of thy kine, and the flocks of thy sheep, in the land which he sware unto thy fathers to give thee.* Deuteronomy 7:13

That I will give you the rain of your land in his due season, the first rain and the latter rain, that thou mayest gather in thy corn, and thy ***wine****, and thine oil.* Deuteronomy 11:14

Israel then shall dwell in safety alone: the fountain of Jacob shall be upon a land of corn and ***wine****; also his heavens shall drop down dew.* Deuteronomy 33:28

Therefore they shall come and sing in the height of Zion, and shall flow together to the goodness of the LORD, for wheat, and for ***wine****, and for oil, and for the young of the flock and of the herd: and their soul shall be as a watered* *garden; and they shall not sorrow any more at all.* Jeremiah 31:12

For she did not know that I gave her corn, and ***wine****, and oil, and multiplied her silver and gold, which they prepared for Baal.* Hosea 2:8

Yea, the LORD will answer and say unto his people, Behold, I will send you corn, and ***wine****, and oil, and ye shall be satisfied therewith: and I will no more make you a reproach among the heathen.* Joel 2:19

For how great is his goodness, and how great is his beauty! corn shall make the young men cheerful, and ***new wine*** *the maids.* Zechariah 9:17

These texts certainly place *tirosh* in a good light. The question however remains, "What is *tirosh*, what does this Hebrew word represent?" If it represents fermented wine as the readers of the English Bible assume, then the debate is over. We have here an abundance of testimony that this item is approved of God and represents a testimony of his goodness to his people. A careful study of the usage of the word "*tirosh*" in the Hebrew Scriptures shows us that it does not represent wine at all. It represents neither fermented nor unfermented wine. Rather, what it represents is grapes, the actual fruit of the vine. This can be clearly established by a series of arguments.

The first argument that indicates the true nature of *tirosh* lies in the words with which it is associated. The phrase "*corn, wine, and oil*" occurs 19 times in the Authorized Version of the Scriptures. The Hebrew terms are *dagan* (דָּגָן), *tirosh*, and *yitshar* (יִצְהָר). *Dagan* means grain and can refer to various grains such as wheat, corn, barley, millet, etc. *Dagan* therefore refers to the produce of the field, to the various grains that were the products of Hebrew agriculture. *Yitshar* is generally translated as oil. It occurs 22 times in the Hebrew Scriptures. As noted above, it occurs 19 times in the phrase *"corn, wine, and oil."* This should be twenty times because the translators for some inexplicable reason translated *dagan* once as wheat instead of as corn in this phrase (Numbers 18:12). Twice *yitshar* occurs in similar phrases where it is connected with wheat (*bar*—see Joel 2:24) and meal (*ariysah*—see Nehemiah 10:37) respectively in place of *dagan*. *Bar* (בָּר) comes from a root meaning winnowing or threshing and can therefore like *dagan* refer to all sorts of grain. *Ariysah* (עֲרִיסָה) comes from a root meaning to comminute (i.e., grind) and can refer to any kind of meal or flour. These are the only occurrences of *yitshar*. It is never used even once in the context of oil as used in anointing etc. For oil used in sacramental purposes for anointing, for illumination in lamps, where it is spoken of as poured out, where oil is definitely a liquid, the term *shemen* (שֶׁמֶן) is always used. For this reason, as well as because it only occurs in the phrase "*corn, wine, and oil*" where it is always associated with the produce of the field, many commentators translate *yitshar* as fruit. Specifically, it is thought to refer to fruit as growing on trees, what we would call the fruit of the orchard. As such it can refer to olives, figs, pomegranates, etc. This brings us back to our original question, what does *tirosh* mean? And the answer seems clear. *Tirosh*, like grain and orchard fruit, is a solid and not a liquid. Like the other two words with which it is associated in these texts, it represents the produce of the vineyard. *Tirosh* refers not to wine but to the grapes themselves. What we have here is a threefold reference to the various produce of Hebrew agriculture. We have, first of all, grains, the produce of the field. Secondly, we have grapes, the produce of the vineyard. And thirdly, we have olives, figs, etc., the produce of the orchard. This threefold use of the land, with a threefold classification of the produce of the land, is referred to by Nehemiah.

The Fruit of the Vine

"*Restore, I pray you, to them, even this day, their lands, their vineyards, their oliveyards, and their houses, also the hundredth part of the money, and of the corn, the* ***wine****, and the oil, that ye exact of them*" Nehemiah 5:11

Now, these threefold products of the land are all solid and are never portrayed as a liquid. All are the direct produce of the field and are not a manufactured product such as bread, olive oil, wine, etc. *Tirosh* is not wine at all, but only refers to the grapes from which wine is later produced. This is confirmed by the fact that *yayin*, which definitely refers to liquid wine is sometimes associated with *shemen,* which is definitely liquid oil, and *tirosh* is never associated with *shemen*. Similarly, *yayin* is never associated with *yitshar*. These consistent distinctions in use of terms in the Hebrew Scriptures confirms that *tirosh* is exclusively associated with the solid produce of the land.

And this is not all. Not only is *tirosh* consistently associated with the solid produce of the land, but it is also consistently associated with the land itself. A total of nine times *tirosh* is directly associated with the earth. In Genesis 27:28 it is set forth as representing the fatness or the fertility of the earth. In Haggai 1:11 it is represented as suffering with the earth as the latter is afflicted with a drought, a drought that is specifically stated to be called down upon all that the ground brings forth. Now the ground can bring forth grapes but it can hardly bring forth wine, much less fermented wine! In Deuteronomy 7:13 it is specifically called the fruit of the land. Again the fruit of the land is grapes and not some manufactured product such as fermented wine. In Joel 1:10 it is considered as being dried up and withered when the land is wasted. Now, when the land is wasted, the vineyard and its fruit can be considered as withered and dried up, but this would hardly cause the bottles of wine to become dried up. Isaiah 24:7 speaks of *tirosh* mourning when the vine languishes. Now this clearly refers to the grapes suffering when the vines in the vineyard are withering. It would be illogical to think of bottles of wine suffering when the vineyard is in distress. Such references can be multiplied on and on. Several times it is used to represent the increase of the earth. Seven times it is used to represent part of the firstfruits. Ten times it is used to represent the tithes and the offerings of the Lord's people. Now it ought to be obvious that while grapes are logically and necessarily part of the firstfruits of the land, this cannot be applied to wine. The tithes similarly were generally of the direct produce of the land rather than of some manufactured items. Since the Lord was to receive his tithe first, the tithe would logically be of the fruit when it was first gathered, rather than of some product such as fermented wine which would not be available until many months after the harvest.

Thirdly, we would like to note the actions with which *tirosh* is associated. In the following texts it is portrayed as gathered, as eaten, as laid up in heaps, and as found in the cluster.

That I will give you the rain of your land in his due season, the first rain and the latter rain, that thou mayest gather in thy corn, and thy ***wine****, and thine oil.* Deuteronomy 11:14

Thou mayest not eat within thy gates the tithe of thy corn, or of thy ***wine****, or of thy oil, or the firstlings of thy herds or of thy flock, nor any of thy vows which thou vowest, nor thy freewill offerings, or heave offering of thine hand.* Deuteronomy 12:17

And as soon as the commandment came abroad, the children of Israel brought in abundance the firstfruits of corn, ***wine****, and oil, and honey, and of all the increase of the field; and the tithe of all things brought they in abundantly. And concerning the children of Israel and Judah, that dwelt in the cities of Judah, they also brought in the tithe of oxen* *and sheep, and the tithe of holy things which were consecrated unto the LORD their God, and laid them by heaps.* 2 Chronicles 31:5-6

Thus saith the LORD, As the ***new wine*** *is found in the cluster, and one saith, Destroy it not; for a blessing is in it: so will I do for my servants' sakes, that I may not destroy them all.* Isaiah 65:8

Now it is obvious that all these actions relate to a solid and not to a liquid. Wine is not gathered in from the fields and it is drunk rather than eaten. Wine is not found in the cluster and neither is it laid up in heaps. These are descriptions can be properly used with respect to grapes, but hardly of wine. There are however two verses that speak of *tirosh* in a context that seems to suggest a liquid. They are…

The LORD hath sworn by his right hand, and by the arm of his strength, Surely I will no more give thy corn to be meat for thine enemies; and the sons of the stranger shall not drink thy ***wine****, for the which thou hast laboured: But they that have gathered it shall eat it, and praise the LORD; and they that have brought it together shall drink it in the courts of my holiness.* Isaiah 62:8-9

So shall thy barns be filled with plenty, and thy presses shall burst out with ***new wine****.* Proverbs 3:10

In the Isaiah passage *tirosh* is spoken of as being drunk. This certainly seems to denote a liquid, as one does not drink solids. However this is only one text out of many and one must never allow the tail to wag the dog. Scripture must be interpreted by Scripture and an abundance of scriptural witnesses have testified to the fact that *tirosh* cannot be a liquid. The resolution of this issue is actually quite simple. The Hebrew word for drink is "*shathah*" (שָׁתָה). The root meaning of this word is to imbibe. It can mean to drink or to banquet and is translated as both, though usually as to drink. The translators of the Authorized Version, viewing *tirosh* as wine, and therefore as a liquid, logically employed the dominant use of the word and translated it as to drink. However viewing *tirosh* as grapes we see that it is quite permissible to translate *shathah* as referring to persons imbibing on grapes or banqueting on grapes. Since the word does not necessarily imply that *tirosh* is being drunk, this text therefore cannot be used to overthrow the position established by many other texts.

The verse from Proverbs is even simpler to explain in a way consistent with our interpretation. In this text winepresses are said to be bursting out with *tirosh.* All that this means is that there has been a harvest so superabundant that the winepresses are overflowing with grapes ready to be pressed. Neither of these texts present any real difficulty for the interpretation that *tirosh* means grapes and certainly do not require a revision of that view. In fact the Scriptures explicitly state what is pressed out in the winepress to yield wine, and it is *tirosh*. We are told…

Thou shalt sow, but thou shalt not reap; thou shalt tread the olives, but thou shalt not anoint thee with oil; and ***sweet wine*** (tirosh), *but shalt not drink* ***wine*** (yayin). Micah 6:15

The translators have rendered *tirosh* here as sweet wine (the word "sweet" is not present in the Hebrew). This is misleading, inferring that tirosh means new wine. What is actually being taught is that as olives are trodden to yield olive oil, *tirosh* is trodden in the winepress to yield *yayin.* On this we can certainly rest our case.

Having reviewed the testimony of the 37 verses that use *tirosh* in a good sense, and having established that it refers to the fruit of the vine, and therefore as something always to be regarded as a blessing from a gracious God, let us now examine the solitary use of this word "*tirosh*" in a negative context.

The Fruit of the Vine

*Whoredom and **wine*** (yayin) *and **new wine*** (tirosh) *take away the heart.* Hosea 4:11

Three things are mentioned here as having a common property; they take away the heart. The heart is the seat of affections and is that part of our being that is to be totally dedicated to the one, only, and true God. That whoredom or fornication corrupts men and turns them from the true God is the uniform testimony of Scripture. Similarly, the effects of alcoholic wine is to take away the heart and corrupt men from the spiritual service of the true God to the material pleasures and lusts of this life. The two are in fact related, and it is a notorious fact that the use of alcoholic beverages clouds the moral judgment, and under its influence men are far more likely to commit sins of the flesh such as fornication, adultery, etc. That the translators took *yayin* to represent alcoholic wine is clear by the fact that they translated *tirosh* as new wine in contrast to it. To say whoredom, alcoholic wine, and alcoholic wine take away the heart would be an obvious redundancy. But, as we have noted, *tirosh* does not mean wine whether it be new wine, or that which has been fermented. It means grapes, the fruit of the vine. What does this verse mean then? How can grapes take away the heart in the sense that fornication and drunkenness can? I believe that the prophet is listing three vices here that take away the heart and corrupt men from the service of the true God. The three vices are fornication, drunkenness, and gluttony. These three are all vices that indulge the physical senses and corrupt men's hearts from spiritual worship and devotion of the true God. And what food was more likely to be the object of the glutton's lust than the grapes of Palestine? Sweet and succulent, and so abundant that a cluster of them could of necessity require two men to carry it, they were one of the choicest foods of the land.

Although I have taken the above position on this passage, it has to admitted that the text in question is not without its difficulties. This is evident from the fact that it has been subject to a wide range of varying translations. One such variant seems worthy of note and I include it as a possible alternative view of this text. The "*Purified Translation of the Old Testament,*"* translates the passage as *"Whoredom, wine, and drunkenness take away the heart*". To the reader it may seem a leap to go from "*tirosh*" to "*drunkenness*", but surprisingly there is strong traditional support for that rendering. As the translators point out in their notes, there are a number of respected historical translations that support that usage, and they felt that, in dealing with a difficult and controversial text, those translators that were closest, chronologically and culturally, to the original probably got it right. They note that both traditional Greek translations of the Old Testament, such as the Septuagint, as well as modern Greek translations, such as the 1925 British Bible Society version, both render *tirosh* as drunkenness. When one considers that Jerome's Latin Vulgate also rendered it as drunkenness, that constitutes a strong tradition in favor of that view. However, irrespective of what one concludes, the symbolic use of *tirosh* to represent drunkenness does not affect the debate over temperance.

If the use of *tirosh* in the above verse could be proven to be alcoholic wine, it would only serve as a warning against it. As it cannot be proven to mean that, then the entire scriptural testimony of the word "*tirosh*" cannot be used in any way to justify men in even the moderate use of alcoholic wine. Since *tirosh* simply means grapes, the fruit of the vine, it has nothing to say on the subject of the lawfulness of alcoholic wine. What our study however does do is take 37 verses, that to the readers of the English Bible

---

* "*The Purified Translation of the Old Testament*" is a current project of the L. L. Reynolds Foundation.

seem to speak well of wine, and removes them from use in the debate over temperance. Thirty-seven scriptural witnesses that have been used to justify the moderate use of alcoholic wine have been silenced. Dozens of texts, that have been used over and over again to defend the moderate use of alcoholic beverages, have been shown to teach no such doctrine. In that sense the debate has been powerfully affected by this word study.

CHAPTER 4
SHEKAR
שֵׁכָר

This word occurs 23 times in the Hebrew Scriptures. Of these citations, two deal with its use in religious observances and the remaining 21 deal with its use as a common beverage. It is remarkable that its use as a common beverage is consistently warned against. For in all 21 such citations it is used in a context that warns against this item called *shekar*. What is *shekar*? What is this substance that stands in such remarkable contrast to *tirosh* which we have just studied? While *tirosh* was virtually universally praised, this substance is virtually universally condemned. This certainly undermines the proponents of the view that *tirosh* and *shekar* all mean the same thing, can all be translated by synonyms for the same thing, and all stand for fermented wine. The unfortunate translation of this word in the Authorized Version of the Scriptures further compounds the difficulty of establishing its proper meaning. It is translated 20 times as strong drink and once as strong wine. This is not only unfortunate, but just plain irresponsible. There is absolutely no literal grammatical support in the Hebrew for the word strong. This has caused the reader of the English Bible to constantly assume that this word must refer to a powerful drink, a beverage that is a strong intoxicant. In fact the connotation is that it might have been something like our modern liquors, powerful drinks that far exceed the intoxicating powers of mere wine. This is of course totally without any foundation. Modern liquors are the results of using a still to concentrate the alcohol, a technology that was totally unknown to Old Testament Hebrews. All such erroneous notions must be put out of our mind as we approach the study of how the Holy Spirit has used this word in the Scriptures.

Shekar means sweet drink. It is related to the word for sugar used in all the Semitic and even the Indo-European languages. It was a drink that was very high in sugar content. As such it was of course subject to fermentation. In the process of fermentation the yeast organisms turn the sugar into alcohol (ethanol), that is, they consume the sugar and secrete alcohol as waste. However, it would be erroneous to assume from this that it was therefore fermented into a drink of exceptionally high alcohol content. The alcohol content is determined by the resistance of the yeast to the alcohol. When the concentration of the alcohol reaches a specific level, the toxicity (i.e., the poisonous nature) of the alcohol kills the yeast, and the process of further fermentation ceases. There is therefore no basis, either linguistically or scientifically, for considering *shekar* a strong drink with respect to other fermented beverages, such as alcoholic *yayin*.

That the word "*shekar*" generally is used in Scripture as an intoxicating beverage is readily granted. This is clearly the case in light of the frequent, indeed almost universal, condemnation of its use. Such persistent condemnation is inexplicable if *shekar* was simply an innocent sweet beverage akin to our lemonade, fruit juices, or soda. A sampling of its use with the attendant condemnations or warnings with respect to its use is as follows…

Do not drink wine nor ***strong drink****, thou, nor thy sons with thee, when ye go into the tabernacle of the congregation, lest ye die: it shall be a statute for ever throughout your generations.* Leviticus 10:9

This verse is especially interesting. For those who are interested in such things, it is the first mention of *shekar* in the Scriptures and it is a prohibition of its use. Additionally, the context is especially noteworthy. Nadab and Abihu, two of Aaron's sons, have just been struck down by God, in judgment, for offering strange fire before the Lord. That is, they took fire from some unauthorized source, rather than from the altar of burnt sacrifice, to burn incense before the Lord in the Holy Place. And immediately after that incident the Lord gives the above quoted prohibition to Aaron. Most commentators believe that Nadab and Abihu committed their transgression while under the influence of alcoholic beverages. This explains the immediate prohibition of the practice, lest God's judgment burn against his priests again. What is clear is that this is, by logical necessity, a prohibition of the consumption of alcoholic beverages by the priests while in the tabernacle/temple. This establishes that *shekar* can be used to refer to an alcoholic beverage. However, it should not be used to intimate that the priests were allowed to use alcoholic beverages while off duty. The prohibition by an employer of alcohol or drugs in the workplace does not necessarily mean that employees may use them at other times. The prohibition of operating a motor vehicle while under the influence of alcohol does not mean it is acceptable to be intoxicated at other times. Therefore no such conclusion should be drawn from this episode. What is important to consider is the disastrous effects of alcohol on Aaron's sons and the response of God to outlaw, not just intoxication, but all its use in his courts.

And Hannah answered and said, No, my lord, I am a woman of a sorrowful spirit: I have drunk neither wine nor ***strong drink****, but have poured out my soul before the LORD.* 1 Samuel 1:15

The context in this text is that a suffering Hannah has her incoherent prayer and her tears witnessed to by Eli who draws the conclusion that she is inebriated. He rebukes her apparent drunkeness and commands her to put away her wine (*yayin*). In her defense she states that she has taken neither *yayin* nor *shekar*. Again this text does two things. It establishes that *shekar* can represent an intoxicating beverage, and by inference and example it condemns its use.

Wine is a mocker, ***strong drink*** *is raging: and whosoever is deceived thereby is not wise.* Proverbs 20:1.

In this text *shekar* is again coupled with *yayin* and they are both condemned as dangerous and deceitful substances that the wise will avoid. The inference that they are intoxicants to be shunned is clear.

It is not for kings, O Lemuel, it is not for kings to drink wine; nor for princes ***strong drink****. Lest they drink, and forget the law, and pervert the judgment of any of the afflicted.* Proverbs 31:4-5

Again *shekar* and *yayin* are coupled together in mutual condemnation and in a mutual prohibition. The consequence of their use is clearly intoxication and leads to corruptions of the judicial functions of civil magistrates.

Woe unto them that rise up early in the morning, that they may follow ***strong drink****; that continue until night, till wine inflame them!* Isaiah 5:11

Again, a woe or a condemnation is pronounced on those who are given to the use of either *yayin* or *shekar*. Not only the inebriating, but also the addicting nature of these substances is inferred.

Woe unto them that are mighty to drink wine, and men of strength to mingle ***strong drink****.* Isaiah 5:22

The propensity of those given to alcohol to boast of their ability to handle intoxicants, their ability to "*hold their liquor*" is being rebuked here. A condemnation of those whose might consists of their ability to exercise such vices is what is being stated.

But they also have erred through wine, and through ***strong drink*** *are out of the way; the priest and the prophet have erred through* ***strong drink,*** *they are swallowed up of wine, they are out of the way through* ***strong drink;*** *they err in vision, they stumble in judgment.* Isaiah 28:7

The condemnation of and the consequences of the use of intoxicating *yayin* and *shekar* is set forth here in the prophet's rebuke.

Stay yourselves, and wonder; cry ye out, and cry: they are drunken, but not with wine; they stagger, but not with ***strong drink.*** Isaiah 29:9

In this text the inference that *yayin* causes drunkeness and that *shekar* causes one to stumble, as well as the intoxicating nature of these substances is clearly expressed.

What has all this revealed to us about the nature of *shekar*? Two things are clearly taught. One is that *shekar* can, and frequently does, refer to an intoxicating drink. Secondly, that in every instance that it does so it is connected with either a warning against it, or a condemnation of it, or both. The above eight texts could be multiplied with more references. Of the 23 times the word "*shekar*" is used it refers to an alcoholic beverage in a context of warning and/or condemnation a total of 15 times. Six times it is used in reference to Nazarite vows, where its use is prohibited, and twice in the context of religious observances, as part of Israel's sacrificial system of worship. What still remains to be determined is whether *shekar* always refers to an intoxicating drink, or whether it can also refer to a non-alcoholic beverage. We still need to obtain an exact definition of what *shekar* is. To do that we need to examine the other texts where *shekar* is used.

The Fruit of the Vine

The first set of texts that we will examine are those that deal with the Nazarite vow. The basic definition of this vow is found in Numbers 6. The section dealing with wine reads as follows…

And the LORD spake unto Moses, saying, Speak unto the children of Israel, and say unto them, When either man or woman shall separate themselves to vow a vow of a Nazarite, to separate themselves unto the LORD: He shall separate himself from wine and ***strong drink****, and shall drink no vinegar of wine, or vinegar of* ***strong drink****, neither shall he drink any liquor of grapes, nor eat moist grapes, or dried. All the days of his separation shall he eat nothing that is made of the vine tree, from the kernels even to the husk.* Numbers 6:1-4

The word for wine in this passage is *yayin* and *shekar* is the word for strong drink. The vow of the Nazarite involved basically three things—certain dietary requirements involving abstinence from specific foods and beverages, letting his hair and beard grow, and complete ceremonial cleanliness. The Nazarite was to separate himself from the world by these means and live a life of special consecration unto the Lord. We will examine only the first requirement. The dietary requirements included abstinence from *yayin* and *shekar*. We have already seen that *yayin* can mean both the freshly expressed blood of the grape, that is, new wine, as well as the fermented variety. Since this is the case, why is *shekar* added to the prohibition? Commentators who take the position that *shekar* means an intoxicating wine introduce a needless redundancy if they are thinking of wine made from grapes. If they are thinking of wine made from other sources than the grape then it begins to make at least some sense. For it is obvious that all forms of beverage produced from the grape were already forbidden, as well as the grapes themselves, whether fresh moist grapes or dried as raisins. We see that *yayin* was forbidden, and that it denotes, as stated above, both new and fermented wine from the grape. We see that vinegar of *yayin*, that is, vinegar made from grape juice, is also forbidden. (Vinegar is produced by a two step process, both involving micro-organisms. In the first step the fresh sweet juice is fermented by yeast into an alcoholic drink. Then, in a subsequent step, the alcohol is oxidized into acetic acid by certain bacteria.) We then note that even "*liquor of grapes*" is forbidden. This latter prohibition probably refers to the beverage made from steeping in water the residue of the fresh grapes left in the winepress after the juice has been expressed and thus producing a kind of grape juice. The Hebrew word for liquor is "*mishrah*" (מִשְׁרָה) from a root word meaning loosening, and means to macerate, that is, to soften or loosen by soaking, and thus is used for beverages produced by steeping in water. Again this is an unfortunate and misleading translation as it conjures up modern images of powerful intoxicants.

This total prohibition of *yayin* and all its associated beverages, no matter how produced, but all originating from the fruit of the vine, gives us a clear understanding of what *shekar* means. *Shekar* is constantly coupled with *yayin* in these prohibitions. It would seem reasonable that the same prohibitions apply to both. *Shekar* is therefore also a generic word. Its root meaning, as we have noted, is sweet drink, a sugary beverage, and we indeed get our word sugar from this word "*shekar*." It therefore represents a number of sweet fruit juices as well as the fermented wines produced from them. Like *yayin,* it represents both the fresh juice and the fermented wine. Unlike *yayin,* it is produced from other juices than the blood of the grape. It is not made from fruit of the vine. Many commentators have noted that *shekar* was frequently used in the ancient Middle East as a term for date or palm wine. *Shekar* therefore stands for such items as the juice of dates and figs, and the fermented wines produced from them. These wines could of course also be turned into vinegars; and these also were forbidden to the Nazarite. In fact, a case could be made, although it is not explicitly stated in the text, that the Nazarite would be forbidden to consume dates, figs, etc., as much as he was forbidden to consume grapes. The most famous Nazarite in the Bible was John the Baptist, and he certainly excluded such from his diet, sustaining himself with locusts and wild honey.

That *shekar* is a generic term that included both the fresh juice as well as the fermented products of figs, dates, etc., is also supported by the way *shekar* is used in the majority of the texts we have reviewed. The Nazarite vow laid additional restrictions on those who undertook to submit to its requirements. But we have already noted that in every instance where *shekar* is used in a context denoting an alcoholic beverage, it is accompanied by warnings and prohibitions. If ordinary persons were already instructed to avoid alcoholic *shekar* then its introduction into the Nazarite vow would be meaningless. It is because it is a generic term, that includes the fresh juices as well, that it provides an additional requirement for the Nazarite to obey. The Nazarite was forbidden *shekar* as a fresh juice, *shekar* as a fermented wine, *shekar* as a vinegar, and perhaps even the fruit from which *shekar* was derived. It is only by viewing it as a generic term, similar to *yayin,* that all these uses of the word "*shekar*" can be logically and consistently explained. Of the six uses involving the Nazarite vow, two were in the text we have just examined that defined the Nazarite vow. Three are in the angel's instructions to Samson's parents (Judges 13:4,7,14), as Samson was to be a Nazarite from the womb. Again we note that the restrictions on Samson and his mother make no sense if *shekar* is always alcoholic and therefore already forbidden under the texts dealing with alcoholic *shekar*. The final text is…

And I have led you forty years in the wilderness: Ye have not eaten bread, neither have ye drunk wine or ***strong drink****: that ye might know that I am the LORD your God.* Deuteronomy 29:5-6.

This can also be interpreted as a Nazarite text, taking the view that Israel in the wilderness was separated from the nations unto the true God and in a sense a nation of Nazarites.

This now brings us to the final class of texts involving the word "*shekar*," the texts involving its use in Israel's sacrificial system under the ceremonial law. There are only two texts and they read as follows…

And the drink offering thereof shall be the fourth part of an hin for the one lamb: in the holy place shalt thou cause the ***strong wine*** *to be poured unto the LORD for a drink offering.* Numbers 28:7

And thou shalt bestow that money for whatsoever thy soul lusteth after, for oxen, or for sheep, or for wine, or for ***strong drink****, or for whatsoever thy soul desireth: and thou shalt eat there before the LORD thy God, and thou shalt rejoice, thou, and thine household.* Deuteronomy 14:26

These are the only two texts in the entire Scriptures that speak well of *shekar* and allow its use. There are no others. If the Scriptures allow persons to use alcoholic shekar, it will have to be established from one of these two texts. I do not believe that it is possible to establish that argument. One would have to prove that these texts involved alcoholic wine, but we have already established that "*shekar*" is a generic word. Additionally, one would have to prove that permission is given here for what is already prohibited elsewhere. This would involve its proponents in the dilemma of resolving the issue of another apparent contradiction in the Scriptures. Since the drink offering was poured out to the Lord, it does not involve its consumption by the worshipper. This leaves a single text as the only possible support for the view that alcoholic *shekar* is a permissible beverage. And there is absolutely nothing in the context to indicate that it refers to alcoholic *shekar* rather than the sweet juice. In fact everything in the context militates against such an interpretation. First, there is no case for moderation here and without moderation the license to use alcoholic beverages is a prescription for sin and disaster. The worshipper is to eat of his tithes with his family. For any prosperous Israelite this could be a considerable quantity. Secondly, it was to be eaten in the tabernacle/temple precincts, in those precincts where there was an additional prohibition of alcoholic drink (*yayin*) for the priests. It was to be shared with the Levites, who like the priests were religious officers in Israel. It was to be the cause of one's rejoicing before the Lord. Does our rejoicing before the Lord come from spiritual worship or is it the result of an alcohol induced "happy hour"? And even if alcoholic *shekar* was in view here, and I find that inconceivable, it would still not establish its legitimate use as an ordinary beverage apart from religious observances. We are left with the inescapable conclusion that our word study of *shekar* leaves us without any proof for, or the authorization of, the use of alcoholic beverages.

CHAPTER 5
OINOS
οἶνος

The Greek word "*oinos*" is, with a solitary exception (Acts 2:13), the exclusive word used for wine in the New Testament and occurs a total of 32 times in the Greek Scriptures. As noted before, it was used by the Septuagint translators as the Greek equivalent of the Hebrew word "*yayin.*" This is a strong clue as to its meaning and as we shall see, it points us in the right direction. Ten times it portrayed as something that is permitted and to be enjoyed. Ten times it is placed in a context where we are warned against it by either precept or example. And finally it is referred to twelve times in a neutral context where we have no indication of either approval or disapproval.

Let us start with examining those texts that approve of this beverage called *oinos*. As stated above there are ten such texts. Six of these, occurring in four texts (John 2:3,9,10; John 4:46), are in reference to the wine produced by Christ's first miracle at the wedding in Cana. These texts will be dealt with in a subsequent chapter. Two more texts are in a context of the medicinal use of wine. These will also be dealt with in a subsequent chapter on that subject. That leaves two texts to be examined. The first one reads as follows…

It is good neither to eat flesh, nor to drink wine, nor any thing whereby thy brother stumbleth, or is offended, or is made weak. Romans 14:21

This passage has to do with the consumption of food that had been sacrificed to pagan idols. This involves the use of foods that are normally legitimate to consume, but are now questionable because of the implication of reverencing pagan idols through their consumption. This passage should therefore be interpreted in light of a parallel passage in Paul's first epistle to the church in Corinth where he elaborates on this issue.

As concerning therefore the eating of those things that are offered in sacrifice unto idols, we know that an idol is nothing in the world, and that there is none other God but one... Howbeit there is not in every man that knowledge: for some with conscience of the idol unto this hour eat it as a thing offered unto an idol; and their conscience being weak is defiled. But meat commendeth us not to God: for neither, if we eat, are we the better; neither, if we eat not, are we the worse. But take heed lest by any means this liberty of yours become a stumblingblock to them that are weak. For if any man see thee which hast knowledge sit at meat in the idol's temple, shall not the conscience of him which is weak be emboldened to eat those things which are offered to idols; And through thy knowledge shall the weak brother perish, for whom Christ died? But when ye sin so against the brethren, and wound their weak conscience, ye sin against Christ. Wherefore, if meat make my brother to offend, I will eat no flesh while the world standeth, lest I make my brother to offend. 1 Corinthians 8:4,7-13

Paul is teaching that foods offered to idols, including such foods as meat and wine, are legitimate to eat. He also states that it is permissible to eat such foods, even if they have been sacrificed to idols, because the Christian knows that the idol is nothing and he takes the food as a gift from his heavenly Father, who is graciously providing his daily bread. What is not legitimate, according to Paul, is to consume such foods, when it causes a fellow believer to be offended and to stumble in their faith over your alleged act of idolatry. In such circumstances the Apostle commands abstinence. Now this passage establishes clearly that there is a species of wine, a species of *oinos*, that is permissible for Christians to consume. What the passage does not indicate is whether the wine being referred to is new wine or the fermented variety. Since *oinos* is used to translate *yayin*, which stands for both fermented and for new wine, and since we will demonstrate in subsequent arguments that it sometimes definitely refers to new wine and sometimes definitely to fermented wine, we have to allow for both possibilities. Therefore the one thing we can conclude is that without further information this text cannot be used to authorize Christians in the consumption of alcoholic wine.

The second text that refers to *oinos* with approval reads as follows…

And I heard a voice in the midst of the four beasts say, A measure of wheat for a penny, and three measures of barley for a penny; and see thou hurt not the oil and the wine. Revelation 6:6

This is a statement with respect to famine conditions. A measure of wheat is about one quart. For one quart of wheat or flour a man has to pay one denarius, which is about a day's pay. These are indeed famine conditions as who can support a family on a quart of wheat per day? The normal price of wheat was about twelve measures for one denarius, so these prices are astronomical, reflecting an eleven hundred per cent increase in the cost of food. In our study of *tirosh* we noted the common expression in the Hebrew Scriptures, *"the corn, the oil, and the wine."* John is probably referring to this familiar phrase. He is noting that although there will be a severe shortage of corn, that is of grains, the supply of wine and oil will not be affected. If John is paralleling the familiar phrase for his readers, then all he means is that, although the grain harvest will be severely affected, the harvest of grapes and of olives will be spared. And of course if they are spared, then the production and supply of olive oil and of wine will remain the same as usual. Since this limitation of the severity of the judgment of famine is an obvious mercy, we have to say that these articles of food are viewed as a blessing and are spoken of approvingly. However, we have no way of determining what kind of wine is in view. Again, this text is inconclusive as far as any explicit or implied approval of the consumption of alcoholic wine is concerned.

Let us now proceed to examine the texts that are neutral with respect to their attitude towards *oinos*. There are a total of twelve of these. Nine of these twelve have to do with Christ's illustration about old and new wine and wineskins. Two have to do with John the Baptist's status as a Nazarite, and the final one merely lists it as an article of commerce. We will start with the latter which reads…

Alas, alas, that great city Babylon, that mighty city! for in one hour is thy judgment come. And the merchants of the earth shall weep and mourn over her; for no man buyeth their merchandise any more: The merchandise of gold, and silver, and precious stones, and of pearls, and fine linen, and purple, and silk, and scarlet, and all thyine wood, and all manner vessels of ivory, and all manner vessels of most precious wood, and of brass, and iron, and marble, And cinnamon, and odours, and ointments, and frankincense, and ***wine****, and oil, and fine flour, and wheat, and beasts, and sheep, and horses, and chariots, and slaves, and souls of men.* Revelation 18:10-13

Nothing can be gained from this text as it simply lists wine, in the familiar trilogy with corn and oil and a host of other articles, as part of the commerce of the great city of Babylon.

For he shall be great in the sight of the Lord, and shall drink neither ***wine*** *nor strong drink; and he shall be filled* *with the Holy Ghost, even from his mother's womb.* Luke 1:15

In this passage the angel Gabriel is announcing to Zacharias the coming birth of John the Baptist and the text before us places John under the Nazaritic rule. Like Samson, he is to be a life long Nazarite from his mother's womb. It is an interesting passage because the standard formula for the Nazaritic vow from Numbers 6:3 is here rendered in Greek. The word for "*yayin*" is "*oinos*" as expected. And the word for "*strong drink,*" again mistranslated, is "*sikera*" (σίκερα), which is derived from the Hebrew *shekar*. However, since *oinos* is used as the Greek equivalent of *yayin* and because we know that the Nazarites were forbidden the use of both new and of fermented wine, this passage again confirms our interpretation of "*oinos*" as a generic word that represents both kinds of wine. And *sikera*, the transliteration into Greek of the Hebrew word "*shekar*," obviously means the same thing as we have seen *shekar* to mean.

And the Lord said, Whereunto then shall I liken the men of this generation? and to what are they like? They are like unto children sitting in the marketplace, and calling one to another, and saying, We have piped unto you, and ye have not danced; we have mourned to you, and ye have not wept. For John the Baptist came neither eating bread nor drinking ***wine****; and ye say, He hath a devil. The Son of man is come eating and drinking; and ye say, Behold a gluttonous man, and a* ***wine****bibber, a friend of publicans and sinners!* Luke 7:31-34

In this passage Christ has just answered a question received from an imprisoned John the Baptist, and has gone on to eulogize John. The Scriptures then say that the people received his words, but the Pharisees rejected them. Christ then utters this denunciation of their two-facedness and hypocrisy. They refused to follow John and denounced his extreme asceticism and attributed it to a demon. They then in turn denounced Christ, who did not practice that kind of asceticism. Christ, who ate and drank as a normal person, and was not under any Nazarite vow, is denounced as a glutton and a winebibber. Both charges are of course untrue and without any foundation. Christ is showing their hypocrisy, their double standard, and that it is logically impossible to please them. The word for the wine from which John abstained is of course *oinos*, the Greek equivalent of *yayin*, and represents both kinds of wine. The word for winebibber that the Pharisees sought to apply to Christ is *oinopotes*, (οἰνοπότης) from *oinos* for wine and *pino* (πίνω) or *pio* (πίω) which means to imbibe. All that it literally implies is a drinker of *oinos*. How the Pharisees meant it is not clear from the text. They could have simply meant that he was a glutton who ate prodigious meals and consumed large quantities of new wine as part of his gluttony. Or they could have meant an implied charge of drunkeness as well as gluttony, considering him a frequent imbiber of fermented wine. Whatever they meant by it is not really germane, because we know that the charge was baseless and Christ exposes its falsity. From other passages of Scripture we know that Christ drank new wine and that in itself is enough to account for the contrast with John the Baptist and the attempt by the Pharisees to slander him. There is nothing here that establishes that Christ used fermented wine, or to authorize his followers to do so.

We now come to the final set of texts that use *oinos* in a neutral context. This passage occurs in the three synoptic gospels. We will use the Luke passage as it contains an additional verse on which we need to comment. Luke's account reads as follows…

And they said unto him, Why do the disciples of John fast often, and make prayers, and likewise the disciples of the Pharisees; but thine eat and drink And he said unto them,

Can ye make the children of the bridechamber fast, while the bridegroom is with them? But the days will come, when the bridegroom shall be taken away from them, and then shall they fast in those days. And he spake also a parable unto them; No man putteth a piece of a new garment upon an old; if otherwise, then both the new maketh a rent, and the piece that was taken out of the new agreeth not with the old. And no man putteth new ***wine*** *into old bottles; else the new* ***wine*** *will burst the bottles, and be spilled, and the bottles shall perish. But new* ***wine*** *must be put into new bottles; and both are preserved. No man also having drunk old wine straightway desireth new: for he saith, The old is better.* Luke 5:33-39

In this passage the Pharisees are again attempting to find fault with Jesus. Again they compare him with John, as well as his disciples with. John's Again, they are being hypocritical because they appear to champion John and his disciples when in fact they rejected John as well as Christ. Christ personally did fast and pray and the record in the gospels of his prayer life is a great example to us. However, neither Christ nor his disciples fasted as frequently and apparently to the same extent as John and his disciples. Jesus explains the reason for this. But there is more to these questions of the Pharisees than simply an innocent question about the differences between John and Christ. Christ therefore goes on to tell a little parable, a parable that illustrated an additional reason for the difference and concluded with a warning to his hearers against the doctrines of the Pharisees. In this parable Christ is comparing the two dispensations, the Jewish and the Christian. He is comparing the Old Testament economy, under the covenant made with Israel at Sinai, with the New Covenant that he is about to institute in his own blood. He first compares them as two garments. He states that one does not patch an old worn-out garment with a piece of cloth taken from a new robe. The effect is to tear the new robe and the patch will not match the old robe anyway. What Jesus is doing is explaining the most significant reason why he and his disciples differ from John and his disciples. Jesus is saying that his teachings, that the doctrines of the New Covenant, cannot be fastened onto the old dispensation like a patch. Particularly, they cannot be fastened onto the religious system that the interpretations and the traditions of the Pharisees have made of the faith of the Old Testament. To attempt to force his teachings into the mold of contemporary Judaism will simply tear or distort them, and anyway, they do not match. The inference is clear. The old robe should be discarded and the new robe should be kept whole and not sacrificed in a vain attempt to salvage the old. The Pharisees should set aside all the doctrines and traditions of men as well as all the typical and ceremonial aspects of the Old Covenant and follow the teachings of Christ.

Secondly, Christ takes up another illustration to repeat the same point. In this illustration Christ's teachings are represented under the figure of new wine. The religious system of Judaism is represented by old wineskins. The results are the same. In the previous illustration both robes are ruined. Here both the new wine and the old wineskin are lost. The inference here is that the new wine has yet to undergo fermentation. When it does it will build up pressure from the carbon dioxide gas released by the process and the old wineskin, being weak, cracked, and dried out, will burst. To try to force the teachings of Christ into the system of doctrine of the Pharisees is an act of folly that will simply destroy both. Christ's new wine must be put into new wineskins. Christ's teachings require a new dispensation, a new religious establishment, the founding of a new church, with new sacraments, etc. Therefore the Pharisees should not expect Jesus and his disciples to conform to their traditions. They have something better, they have a new garment, they have new wine.

Now, it is obvious that in all this there is nothing that can be construed as an authorization for Christians to consume old or fermented wine. In both illustrations Christ is teaching that the old is inferior and that the new is better. The new garment is better than the old one that needs patching. The new wine is better than the old wineskin. Christ is not teaching here with respect to the issue of temperance, and it is not legitimate to seek to draw inferences on that subject from this passage. However, any inferences that are drawn would necessarily favor new wine over the old. This is brought out even more emphatically in the final verse. Christ is here criticizing the Pharisees and their disciples. They are rejecting the new wine. They think the old wine is better. They have drunk too deeply of the doctrines of Judaism. They see nothing wrong with their current beliefs. They see no need to change. At best they may agree to patch the old garment, but discard it…never! Christ is issuing a warning here. He is warning his hearers against imbibing too deeply of the doctrines of the scribes and Pharisees, as he warned elsewhere when he said...

Take heed and beware of the leaven of the Pharisees and of the Sadducees…Then understood they how that he bade them not beware of the leaven of bread, but of the doctrine of the Pharisees and of the Sadducees. Matthew 16:6,12

Again, we should not make any inferences here with respect to the issue of temperance. However, for those who insist on doing so, and who interpret this passage to say that Christ is teaching that old or fermented wine is better, we say that they are wrong. If anything, Christ is attributing that error to the Pharisees, while he himself is teaching that new wine is better. As with the texts that spoke approvingly of *oinos,* we see no support here for the doctrine that the Scriptures authorize the disciples of Jesus Christ to consume alcoholic wine as a normal beverage. All these texts are, at best, silent with respect to that question. We are now ready to proceed with an examination of the texts that use *oinos* in a context of disapproval, prohibition, or warning.

Of the ten texts that deal with *oinos* in a negative context of disapproval, six are in the book of Revelation, where they used in a symbolic and figurative sense. Two additional texts involve prohibitions of being "*given to much wine.*" An additional text is possibly intended in a medicinal sense, and finally there is another text with a prohibition. We will examine them all in turn but will leave the medicinal use text (Mark 15:23) to the chapter on that subject. We will deal with the three texts that deal with actual wine first and then the symbolic texts from the Revelation. These texts read as follows…

Redeeming the time, because the days are evil Wherefore be ye not unwise, but understanding what the will of the Lord is. And be not drunk with ***wine****, wherein is excess; but be filled with the Spirit; Speaking to yourselves in psalms and hymns and spiritual songs, singing and making melody in your heart to the Lord; Giving thanks always for all things unto God and the Father in the name of our Lord Jesus Christ.* Ephesians 5:16-20

Paul has just warned that the days are evil. This evil consists, in part, of intoxication through alcoholic wine. Paul warns that such wine contains "*excess*" (asotia - ἀσωτία), which could be translated debauchery. Paul is not speaking of excess of wine. He is referring to the "excess" or "debauchery" that is contained in alcoholic wine. Paul is warning against drunkeness from alcoholic wine, which contains debauchery. Paul does not offer moderation as a solution to this danger. Rather, he states that in place of being filled with alcoholic wine we ought to be filled with the Spirit of God. Rather than coming under the influence of alcoholic wine wherein is debauchery we ought to come under the influence of the Holy Spirit. The result of this will stand in deep contrast with the results of alcoholic wine, which is debauchery. Under the influence of the Spirit we will sing praises to God and have a heart full of thankfulness.* All this text contains is a strong admonition to avoid alcoholic wine. There is no case here for moderate use of such wine and no authorization for its use. Rather we are warned that such wine contains the power to seduce into debauchery.

Paul in the next two texts utters additional warnings and prohibitions with respect to alcoholic wine.

Likewise must the deacons be grave, not doubletongued, not given to much ***wine****, not greedy of filthy lucre.* 1 Timothy 3:8

The aged women likewise, that they be in behaviour as becometh holiness, not false accusers, not given to much ***wine****, teachers of good things.* Titus 2:3

Paul is speaking here of alcoholic wine. This is manifest from the context. He forbids certain classes of hearers to be given to much wine. What is meant in these verses by the phrase "*given to*"? It means to be addicted to. This is especially apparent from the word used in the Titus passage. It is *douloo* (δουλόω), which means to be enslaved. Now, people generally are not addicted to new wine, but are addicted to alcohol, which is only in fermented wine. Also, much has been made of the "*much*" in the phrase "*much wine.*" This has been interpreted as prohibiting only excess

---

* The Greek words for psalms, hymns, and spiritual songs are the words that the Septuagint translators used to translate the Hebrew words for the names of the various types of songs in the Book of Psalms. Being filled with the Spirit will have the opposite effect of being filled with wine. It will cause us to praise God and sing the songs of the Spirit, the divinely inspired psalms, and will fill our hearts with thankfulness to God rather than with rebellion against God fueled by the dissipation of alcohol.

of wine and permitting moderate use. This is, however, to misunderstand the Apostle. Paul is not merely prohibiting large quantities of wine, and neither is he merely censuring drunkeness. The quantity of the wine is not the issue here. What Paul is prohibiting is to be addicted to wine. How does one avoid becoming addicted to alcoholic wine? The best way and the only sure way is to avoid alcoholic wine altogether. Predisposition to alcohol addiction varies with the individual and can be genetically disposed. One should not tempt God and see how much alcoholic wine one can use and remain unaddicted. The true path of obedience would be to avoid all temptation in this regard and avoid addictive substances whenever such addiction is so strictly proscribed. Neither should we argue that this admonition is only for elders, deacons, and aged women and that all others are allowed to "*be given to wine.*" That is an obvious absurdity. That is just as absurd as the principle alleged by some that prohibition or condemnation of excess equals permission for moderate use. We will deal with that error in the chapter on objections.

Finally, the parallel passage with respect to elders reads...

*Not given to **wine**, no striker, not greedy of filthy lucre; but patient, not a brawler, not covetous.* 1 Timothy 3:3

In this passage the phrase "*given to wine*" is translated from a single Greek word "*paroinos*" (πάροινος), which means staying near wine. If elders are forbidden to stay near alcoholic wine, they are by clear and necessary inference to stay away from alcoholic wine. This is an admonition for abstinence and not a prescription for moderate use.

We are now ready to examine the figurative uses of *oinos* in the Revelation. There are six of these texts. Three deal with the wine of the fornication of Babylon and three deal with the wine of the wrath of Almighty God. They read as follows:

And there followed another angel, saying, Babylon is fallen, is fallen, that great city, because she made all nations drink of the ***wine*** *of the wrath of her fornication.* Revelation 14:8

With whom the kings of the earth have committed fornication, and the inhabitants of the earth have been made drunk with the ***wine*** *of her fornication.* Revelation 17:2

For all nations have drunk of the ***wine*** *of the wrath of her fornication, and the kings of the earth have committed fornication with her, and the merchants of the earth are waxed rich through the abundance of her delicacies.* Revelation 18:3

The same shall drink of the ***wine*** *of the wrath of God, which is poured out without mixture into the cup of his indignation; and he shall be tormented with fire and brimstone in the presence of the holy angels, and in the presence of the Lamb.* Revelation 14:10

And the great city was divided into three parts, and the cities of the nations fell: and great Babylon came in remembrance before God, to give unto her the cup of the ***wine*** *of the fierceness of his wrath.* Revelation 16:19

And out of his mouth goeth a sharp sword, that with it he should smite the nations: and he shall rule them with a rod of iron: and he treadeth the ***wine****press of the fierceness and wrath of Almighty God.* Revelation 19:15

Wine is used symbolically in these texts in two different senses. The first refers to the wine of Babylon. Whether this refers to literal Babylon or some other city that has become a center for false religion and the epitome of corruption and wickedness in the sight of God is not our concern here. What John is saying is that even as alcoholic wine is known to loosen the inhibitions, relax moral restraints, and induce into fornication, even so does the wine of Babylon induce those nations under her influence to forsake the true God and partake in her idolatrous system of worship. God's response to the wine of Babylon is to pour out his own wine, which symbolizes his wrath on all such wickedness and idolatry. Since these texts are highly figurative and symbolic, it would not be wise to attempt to make arguments from them with respect to the issue of temperance. We have sufficient texts that deal with wine as wine to construct our doctrine with respect to the use of alcoholic wine. What we can say is that these texts do not encourage us in the consumption of wine, especially in the consumption of alcoholic wine, as the reference to the wine of Babylon clearly infers its intoxicating power over the nations. Similarly, drinking the cup of the wine of the wrath of Almighty God is more akin to the drinking of powerful wines in its destructive effects on the recipients, than a cup of new wine, that the Scriptures set forth as a blessing of God and a testimony of his bounty to his creatures. We do not need these texts to form our doctrine and are comfortable to let them speak solely the spiritual message that they convey. However, if anyone insists on adding them into the debate, they clearly come down on the side of abstinence from alcoholic wine.

And here we rest our case with respect to our study of the word "*oinos*." We find in our examination of this word and its usage not the slightest support for, or authorization of, the use of alcoholic wine by the Lord's people. If that is to be justified by the Scriptures, it cannot be done by the texts that use the word "*oinos*" for wine. These texts only confirm us in the doctrine that the Scriptures teach us to abstain from such beverages.

CHAPTER 6
A WEDDING AT CANA

Previously, we deferred the discussion of *oinos* as used with reference to the wine miraculously produced at the wedding at Cana. This is the place where we intend to pick up the discussion of that issue. The question before us, the issue that we need to grapple with, is "What kind of wine was produced by Christ at that wedding?" That is, what was the real nature of Christ's first public miracle.

The narrative as recorded by the Evangelist John states that Mary, Jesus, and his disciples were all guests at this wedding. At least one of the families involved in the wedding were probably relatives of Mary or Joseph, and therefore they were all invited. Cana was a village of Galilee and a fairly insignificant one. The importance of this will be pointed out later. Through its lack of importance it has in a sense ceased to exist and we do not even know where it was. There are two rival sites, both consisting of Arab villages, that vie for the distinction of being the site of Christ's first miracle.

As we have already noted, *oinos* can mean both new as well as fermented wine. Again, we must examine the context to see if we can determine what kind of wine this was. And again, in God's good providence, we do not lack clues to definitively establish the nature of this wine. As we embark on this investigation it is important to remember the issue before us. All Christians agree that excessive use of wine to the point of coming under its influence is forbidden. All Christians agree that any degree of intoxication is sin. How this miracle relates to the issue of temperance will be settled by whether its circumstances point to abstinence or whether they are consistent with the principle of moderate use. These two positions are the only ones possible for any Christian to accept. We will establish that it is impossible to reconcile the circumstances of this miracle with the principle of moderate use, if alcoholic wine is what was produced by our Lord.

The first thing we have to note is that the wedding was originally supplied with wine. However, at some point in the wedding feast, which in Jewish tradition lasted for several days, they ran out of wine. This became the occasion for Christ's first miracle, the turning of water into wine. At that point, however, the guests had already been drinking wine. Our first clue is therefore just that, for the text tells us…

When the ruler of the feast had tasted the water that was made wine, and knew not whence it was: (but the servants which drew the water knew;) the governor of the feast called the bridegroom, And saith unto him, Every man at the beginning doth set forth good wine; and when men have well drunk, then that which is worse: but thou hast kept the good wine until now. John 2:9-10

The governor of the feast is complaining because he thinks that the best wine has been reserved until later in the feast. He states that men ought to put out the best wine first and only after the guests have filled up on that to introduce the inferior wine. He complains that they have waited until the guests have filled up on the poorer wine before setting forth the best. The actual Greek word used for the phrase "*well drunk*" is "*methuo*" (μεθύω). It means to drink well. In a context of alcoholic wine it means to drink to the point of drunkeness. It is therefore related to the Greek words for drunken and drunkard. *Methuo* occurs seven times in the New Testament, and in five of the other six times it refers to drunkeness.* What it means in the context of the governor's speech is that the guests had already generously imbibed of the inferior wine before the superior wine was set forth. Now we are compelled to ask, "What kind of wine did the governor have in mind when he said this?" Did he mean that the guests had already generously partaken of new wine and now, when they were already filled up, the best wine is being offered to them? Or did he actually mean that the guests were already proceeding to get drunk on alcoholic wine when the better wine was presented? Was he saying that the guests have been allowed to get drunk on "cheap wine," and now that they were half drunk and couldn't tell the difference, the best wine was being set out for them? Are we to believe that Christ, and his mother, and his disciples attended a wedding feast which was proceeding to degenerate into a drunken festival? Can we really believe this of him of whom the Scriptures testify that he was holy, harmless, and undefiled, and separate from sinners? Did Christ violate the command of Scripture that said,

Hear thou, my son, and be wise, and guide thine heart in the way. Be not among winebibbers... Proverbs 23:19-20

There is really no case for moderate drinking of fermented wine here. Either the guests have "*well drunk*" of new wine, the innocent blood of the grape, or they are getting drunk on alcoholic wine. The text gives us no other alternatives. We are compelled to the conclusion that it had to be new wine. We are confirmed in this interpretation by

---

* The only other exception is 1 Corinthians 11:21 where Paul condemns the Corinthians for not sharing their meals so that while the more prosperous were eating and drinking to excess, others were hungry and thirsty. It is unlikely that they were drinking alcoholic wine and actually becoming drunken in church. If they were actually becoming drunken Paul would have most certainly rebuked them for that, instead of merely commenting on the inequities of the situation. If the effect of excessive drinking was not drunkeness, then the beverage used had to be non-alcoholic.

another fact of the circumstances. The text informs us that Christ produced a considerable quantity of wine.

And there were set there six waterpots of stone, after the manner of the purifying of the Jews, containing two or three firkins apiece. Jesus saith unto them, Fill the waterpots with water. And they filled them up to the brim. And he saith unto them, Draw out now, and bear unto the governor of the feast. And they bare it. John 2:6-8

The precise amount came to somewhere between twelve and eighteen firkins. How much is a firkin? A firkin is an archaic English unit of measure. The Greek word is "*metretes*" (μετρητής). It means a measurer and refers to a specific Greek unit of liquid measure. I have consulted about half a dozen Bible dictionaries for an estimate of what this measure is. Their estimates range from eight and one-half gallons to ten gallons. What this means is that Christ produced a quantity of no less than 100 gallons of wine and possibly as much as 180 gallons. Now, again we must ask, "What kind of wine was this?" Are we to believe that when the guests were already beginning to get drunk that Christ miraculously produced an additional 100-180 gallons of intoxicating wine? Are we to believe that by his first public miracle Christ enabled a drunken party to carry on? Are we to believe that Christ by his first miracle placed himself under a Biblical curse? For the Scriptures teach…

Woe to him who gives drink to his neighbor, Pressing him to your bottle, Even to make him drunk, That you may look on his nakedness! Habakkuk 2:15 (NKJV)

If Christ encouraged drunkeness at this wedding by placing before the guests over 100 gallons of intoxicating wine, it would have brought him under the above noted condemnation of the prophet Habakkuk. We cannot believe such a thing. It is impossible. The Scriptures say at the conclusion of this passage that by this miracle Christ, "*manifested forth his glory.*" That conclusion is totally inconsistent with the facts of the case if we presume that the wine produced by Christ was fermented.

If Christ produced well over 100 gallons of additional alcoholic wine after the guests had already had plenty to drink, this would be no prescription for moderate use of alcoholic beverages. It would be a prescription for, an invitation to, drunkenness. Even if it had been a very large wedding with hundreds of guests, that would still have left at least one-half gallon of alcoholic wine per adult guest. However, Cana was only a country village and the wedding party, in all likelihood, was of modest size. It is far more likely that there would have been an additional gallon or more of alcoholic wine per adult guest. It is not conceivable that Christ would have done such a thing. The case for moderate use of alcoholic beverages simply does not fit the facts as presented in the sacred text. We can rest assured that Christ produced a generous quantity of simple, innocent, harmless, new wine that the guests could enjoy to the full without any implications of sin.

CHAPTER 7
COMMUNION WINE

One of the key issues with respect to the question of temperance is the issue of communion wine. All acknowledge that wine was used at the Last Supper. The question that is in dispute is, "What kind of wine was it?". Was it new wine or was it fermented wine? The text does not explicitly tell us. As we have noted the word "*oinos*" can mean either kind of wine, but the word "wine" (*oinos*) does not even appear in any of the accounts of the Last Supper. For these reasons, we need all the more to carefully study the context to determine what kind of wine was used. First of all, we need to note that the Lord's Supper was instituted at a time when Christ and his disciples were observing the Passover. This will provide us with valuable information as to the nature of the wine that was used. What they were actually observing was the Feast of the Passover, which lasted for seven days. The basic law of this feast, also called in Scripture the Feast of Unleavened Bread*, is found in Exodus 12. The relevant portion for our purposes is quoted below.

Seven days shall ye eat unleavened bread; even the first day ye shall put away leaven out of your houses: for whosoever

---

* The word "Bread" is not in the original Greek. The texts that speak of the "*Feast of Unleavened Bread*" actually only say the "Feast of Unleavened." This is unfortunate because it creates the false assumption that the only leaven that the Jews were concerned about was in the bread. Actually all leaven was forbidden in this feast. The Purified Translation of the New Testament (L. L. Reynolds Foundation, 702 Custis Road, Glenside, PA 19038) therefore more accurately translates this phrase as the "*Feast of Unleavened Things.*"

eateth leavened bread from the first day until the seventh day, that soul shall be cut off from Israel...Seven days shall there be no leaven found in your houses: for whosoever eateth that which is leavened, even that soul shall be cut off from the congregation of Israel, whether he be a stranger, or born in the land. Ye shall eat nothing leavened; in all your habitations shall ye eat unleavened bread. Exodus 12:15,19-20

A fundamental requirement of this feast was that there should be no leaven in the home at all. The emphasis was on the absence of leavened bread. This is undoubtedly because leavened bread was the chief, and perhaps the only, source of leaven in a typical Israelite's home. If so, this becomes an additional argument that alcoholic wine was not in normal use among godly Israelites. It could also be that, as slaves in Egypt, they were fed a diet that did not include any wine. Leavened bread would then have been the only source of leaven that they had to concern themselves with. At any rate the faithful observance of the festival requires the removal of all leaven or yeast from the home. And the two chief sources of leaven, in fact the only sources of leaven that I can think of, are the leaven in leavened bread and in fermented wine. This should be obvious to all, but inexplicably, that has not been the case.

It is agreed to, almost universally, that unleavened bread was used at the Passover. Therefore it is agreed to by all that unleavened bread was used by Christ and his disciples at the Last Supper. Yet strangely enough the same argument has not been applied to the wine. If no yeast was allowed to even be in the house, how could fermented beverages be allowed? It is yeast that causes new wine to ferment into alcoholic wine. But yeast was forbidden to even be in the house! One could argue that the yeast was dead and therefore, in a sense, no yeast was in the wine. However, this is untrue and does not meet the clear scriptural requirements. There was yeast in leavened bread and so it is forbidden. The yeast is put into the dough and causes it to rise. When it is risen sufficiently, it is baked. The baking process kills the yeast. But the dead yeast remains in the bread and therefore the bread is forbidden, not only to be eaten, but its very presence in the house is unlawful during the entire feast of the Passover. Now when the process of fermentation is complete, there is yeast in the wine. If the wine has reached the maximum concentration of alcohol and the resulting toxicity has killed the yeast, then the dead yeast remains in the wine. Then, like the leavened bread, it is excluded by the law of the Passover. If the process of fermentation has gone to completion another way, that is, the sugar has been depleted before a lethal concentration of alcohol has killed the yeast, then the wine continues to contain living yeast. Either way, the wine is excluded from use during the Passover and its presence in the house is illegal! Are we to believe that Christ and his disciples, preparing to observe the Passover, broke the most fundamental law of this feast? Are we to believe that on the eve of the atonement they sinned and violated the requirements of this festival? We can come to no other conclusion than that, by the fundamental law of the Passover, the wine used at the Last Supper was new wine, was non-fermented, and therefore contained no yeast.

We could rest our case right here and be confident of our position, but there is much more that can be said to clearly, convincingly, and in our opinion overwhelmingly prove that new wine was what Christ used at the Last Supper. Next we read that Christ took the cup and blessed it. Did Christ bless that which he was forbidden to even look at with desire? Solomon instructs us…

*Look not thou upon the wine when it is red, when it giveth his colour in the cup, when it moveth itself aright.** *At the last it biteth like a serpent, and stingeth like an adder.* Proverbs 23:31-32

How could something that we are forbidden to even observe with desire become a necessary ingredient in one of the church's sacraments, a sacrament that we are commanded to perform? We are to look forward to the observance of the Lord's Supper. We are to desire the spiritual blessings that accompany the worthy partaking of the bread and the wine. How can we do that if we are simultaneously forbidden to desire the very elements of the sacrament? This is a contradiction that the proponents of alcoholic communion wine will have to resolve.

Then we come to the actual consumption of this communion wine by Christ and the disciples. Could Christ actually have consumed alcoholic wine? The clear and compelling scriptural testimony is no. For again we have to consider the words of Solomon telling us...

It is not for kings, O Lemuel, it is not for kings to drink wine; nor for princes strong drink: Lest they drink, and forget the law, and pervert the judgment of any of the afflicted. Proverbs 31:4-5

Now Christ was a king. Can any Christian dispute this? He is not just any king but he is King of Kings, and Lord of Lords, and Prince of the Kings of the earth. And as a king he was forbidden to partake of alcoholic wine. Are we to believe that Christ sinned as he was preparing to go to the cross? Are we to believe, that as he was observing the

---

* The phrase "*moveth itself aright*" probably has reference to the effervescence of fermentation, as can be observed in the bubbly, sparkling nature of such alcoholic beverages as champagne. This is another confirmation that the text is definitely referring to alcoholic wine.

Passover, which, typified him as the sinless, spotless, Lamb of God, he was actually ,transgressing the commandments with respect to alcoholic wine? In a few hours Christ would be interrogated at his trials before the Sanhedrin, Herod, and Pilate. There he confessed that he was a king.

And Jesus stood before the governor: and the governor asked him, saying, Art thou the King of the Jews? And Jesus said unto him, Thou sayest. Matthew 27:11

The implication of Christ's response is clearer in more modern translations.

Now Jesus stood before the governor. And the governor asked Him, saying, "Are You the King of the Jews?" Jesus said to him, "It is as you say." Matthew 27:11 (NKJV)

Christ affirms here that he was a king. Accordingly Pilate had a superscription placed on the cross identifying him as the King of Israel. The Pharisees sought to change this, but Pilate refused.

And Pilate wrote a title, and put it on the cross. And the writing was, JESUS OF NAZARETH THE KING OF THE JEWS. This title then read many of the Jews: for the place where Jesus was crucified was nigh to the city: and it was written in Hebrew, and Greek, and Latin. Then said the chief priests of the Jews to Pilate, Write not, The King of the Jews; but that he said, I am King of the Jews. Pilate answered, What I have written I have written. John 19:19-22

Pilate's legal testimony to the truth was always providentially preserved as part of the historic record. His frequent testimonies to Christ's innocence, as well as his testimony that Jesus of Nazareth was the King of the Jews, is faithfully recorded in the Scriptures. As Nathaniel confessed when he first met the omniscient Christ…

Nathanael answered and saith unto him, Rabbi, thou art the Son of God; thou art the King of Israel. John 1:49

But the passage in Proverbs clearly states that Christ, as a king, was forbidden to partake of alcoholic wine!

It is not for kings, O Lemuel, it is not for kings to drink wine; nor for princes strong drink: Lest they drink, and forget the law, and pervert the judgment of any of the afflicted. Proverbs 31:4-5

And if Christ did not violate this commandment, then we know that the wine used at the Last Supper was not alcoholic wine. Now, some may say that Christ himself did not partake of the Lord's Supper. The accounts do suggest that Christ blessed the elements and then gave them to his disciples to eat and to drink. In fact, Christ specifically stated of the wine as he distributed the cup, that they were to drink all of it, and that he would not drink of it until the kingdom of God should come. However this does not weaken our argument at all. First of all, Christ instituted the Lord's Supper at the end of their meal. All agree that he used the common elements of their meal to institute this sacrament of the New Covenant. Now Christ had partaken of the this meal with his disciples. He himself testifies to this saying…

With desire I have desired to eat this passover with you before I suffer: For I say unto you, I will not any more eat thereof, until it be fulfilled in the kingdom of God. Luke 22:15-16

This is a very explicit statement. Jesus strongly emphasized his purpose to partake of this meal, as the Greek literally says "*with desire I have desired to eat this Passover.*" And when is this to take place? It is before he suffers. Christ then adds that this will be his last Passover with his disciples and that he will not partake of it again until it is all fulfilled in the Kingdom of God. Similarly Paul says...

After the same manner also he took the cup, when he had supped, saying, This cup is the new testament in my blood: this do ye, as oft as ye drink it, in remembrance of me. 1 Corinthians 11:25

Paul is saying that when Christ had personally partaken of the Passover meal, then he took the cup and instituted the sacrament. Therefore, whatever elements were used in the Lord's Supper, they were the same as were consumed by Christ and his disciples in the Last Supper, their last Passover meal in this world. And we know that Christ, as the true King of Israel, did not drink any alcoholic wine. Therefore we are certain that the wine used at the Last Supper was new wine, the fresh blood of the grape, representing his blood, about to be shed as an atonement for sin.

This interpretation is confirmed by three facts. First Christ refers to the communion wine as the fruit of the wine.

But I say unto you, I will not drink henceforth of this fruit of the vine, until that day when I drink it new with you in my Father's kingdom. Matthew 26:29

Now, the clear connotation of this reference is that it is new wine, grape juice freshly expressed from the fruit of the vine. It is somewhat of a stretch to interpret this as a manufactured product produced many months after the grapes have ceased to exist. Secondly, this very communion wine, that he is offering to his disciples, is the very same wine that he will drink with them again in the Kingdom of God. At that time he will have entered into his kingdom. At that time he will be more a king then ever before. Who will believe that he will then partake of a wine forbidden to kings? And finally Christ confirms this interpretation by his actions on the cross. On the cross he refused to accept any alcoholic wine.

And they bring him unto the place Golgotha, which is, being interpreted, The place of a skull. And they gave him to drink wine mingled with myrrh: but he received it not. Mark 15:22-23

What Christ was refusing here was mixed wine. This consists of alcoholic wine with additional drugs and spices mixed in to enhance and compound its intoxicating effects. This particular wine was mingled with myrrh. Mixed wine, as defined above, is always condemned in the Scriptures. The intended use of this mixture was to act as a narcotic or an anesthetic. As such, this was an act of mercy by the Roman soldiers, because they knew the terrible suffering that they were about to inflict on those to be crucified. Christ however refused it. Why did he do so? There are two obvious reasons. One of these has already been alluded to, that as a king such wine was specifically forbidden to him. Secondly, he came to suffer and to pay the full penalty for all the sins of his people. He would drink to the full, to the very dregs, the bitter cup of suffering that the Father was pouring out for him. The use of this wine might possibly have been allowed under the medicinal use of wine as mentioned in the Proverbs.

Give strong drink (*shekar*) *to him who is perishing, And wine* (yayin) *to those who are bitter of heart.* Proverbs 31:6

In spite of this, Christ was determined to make a full atonement of our sins and to pay the price for all of our transgressions. Therefore he refused any mitigation of his suffering. He refused the drugged alcoholic wine. But he accepted wine vinegar, which is non-alcoholic.

After this, Jesus knowing that all things were now accomplished, that the scripture might be fulfilled, saith, I thirst Now there was set a vessel full of vinegar: and they filled a sponge with vinegar, and put it upon hyssop, and put it to his mouth. When Jesus therefore had received the vinegar, he said, It is finished: and he bowed his head, and gave up the ghost. John 19:28-30

Christ was a king. He never drank any alcoholic wine. He could not have taken any alcoholic wine at the Last Supper. There could not even have been any alcoholic wine in the house during the feast of the Passover. Therefore Christ and his disciples used non-alcoholic wine at the institution of the Lord's Supper. Therefore communion wine by precedent and by the example of our Lord ought to be non-alcoholic wine.

At the Last Supper Christ taught, "*I am the true vine*" (John 15:1). This completes the imagery of the Lord's Supper. We drink of the fruit of the vine, the blood of the grape, representing the blood of Jesus Christ shed for a complete remission of all our sins. The drinking of new wine, of fresh grape juice, perfectly fits these analogies. As soon as we begin to speak of fermented wine, the perfect parallels disappear and the imagery becomes corrupted. Logically and typically, we ought to use new wine as a symbol of the atoning blood of our Lord. And furthermore, we might ask, how can something that has become corrupted with a toxic chemical be the symbol for a life-giving nourishing drink representing the atoning blood of Jesus Christ? How can something that the Apostle Paul under inspiration states contains the principle of debauchery be used to represent the blood of our sinless Lord, the blood of the spotless Lamb of God? Again, these are questions that demand answers, answers that the proponents of alcoholic communion wine are obliged to give us, if they can.

It is interesting that the New Testament accounts of the Last Supper nowhere use the word "*oinos*." The authors deliberately avoided the use of the only word in the New

Testament that can mean alcoholic wine.* The wine is never directly mentioned and the only references made are to the cup. The only exception to this occurs when direct reference is made to the fruit of the vine. This is significant. It is therefore impossible to prove by direct testimony of the Scriptures that fermented wine was used at the Last Supper. If, as many insist, that the Scriptures require the use of fermented wine for the observance of the Lord's Supper, the use of the word "*oinos*" would have cleared the way for that view. It would of course not have established that view, but it would at least have opened the door to that possibility. The total silence of the Scriptures with respect to the use of the only word that can possibly mean alcoholic wine leaves its proponents with a heavy burden of proof. It leaves them with only the possibility of a circumstantial case. And, as we have seen, all the circumstances are actually against their view. This leads us to the certain conclusion that the wine used at the Last Supper was unfermented wine. And if that is the case, that is to be our example. Let us go and do likewise.

---

* That is alcoholic wine made from grapes. The only exception to this is the transliteration into Greek of the Hebrew word *shekar* in Luke 1:15.

CHAPTER 8
MEDICINAL USE

Having considered the question of what the Scriptures teach with respect to the casual or social use of alcoholic beverages, we now go on to examine what they have to say with respect to their medicinal use. Some, who are convinced that the Scriptures teach abstinence from alcoholic beverages want to rigidly exclude all use. They would argue, "What is the medicinal benefit of alcohol, of something that the Scriptures call a poison and compares to the venom of snakes?" However, as we did when we dealt with the issue of temperance itself, we have to examine the Scriptures, and not be guided by our own wisdom, much less by our own preconceptions and prejudices. The Scriptures actually have a number of texts that deal with the medicinal use of wine. We will examine them one by one. And as always, we will have to wrestle with the question of whether the wine so used is new wine or fermented wine. As always, we will have to carefully examine the context and make our evaluations based on the scriptural evidence and the clues provided.

The first passage that we will examine, and the only one in the Old Testament, is a follow-up verse to the prohibition in Proverbs of kings indulging in alcoholic wine. It reads…

It is not for kings, O Lemuel, it is not for kings to drink wine; nor for princes strong drink: Lest they drink, and forget the law, and pervert the judgment of any of the afflicted. Give strong drink unto him that is ready to perish, and wine unto those that be of heavy hearts. Proverbs 31:4-6

Now, in the context here, we can easily determine that alcoholic wine is in view. New wine does not cause men to forget the law and to corrupt justice. Having denied its use to kings, the writer goes on to suggest another use for alcoholic wine. This passage is, frankly speaking, not without its difficulties. However we interpret it, one thing is clear, the intended use of these alcoholic beverages is medicinal. They speak nothing to us concerning normal, social use, of such beverages. It speaks of ministering to those who are at the point of death, and those who are depressed. If the imminent death is a painful one, and the depression is caused by the burden of unrelenting pain, then the medicinal use of alcohol as an anaesthetic or an analgesic is a possible interpretation of this text. Unless we take Solomon to be speaking either symbolically or sarcastically, almost no other literal interpretation is open to us. We will comment more on this issue when we examine the text where Christ refused such alleviation of his pain when he was at the point of death.

The next passage that we want to examine is from one of Christ's parables.

And went to him, and bound up his wounds, pouring in oil and wine (oinos)*, and set him on his own beast, and brought him to an inn, and took care of him.* Luke 10:34

This passage deals with the actions of the Good Samaritan in the parable of that name. Having found a severely wounded traveler, the Good Samaritan proceeds to minister to him. These are medical actions. And part of this medical treatment includes pouring oil and wine into the man's wounds. Now, I am not a doctor, and I hesitate to say what the medicinal value of these actions might be. Particularly, I do not know whether medicinal use gives us a clue as to what kind of wine was used. Fermented wine with a high alcoholic content can act as a disinfectant and have an antibiotic effect. One reads that at times men poured whiskey, etc., into wounds to sterilize them. However, there is a fairly high consensus that the fermented wines of Palestine were not of high alcoholic content. So I am not sure whether they could have been used in that way. However, since we do not know what kind of wine was used, and since it was not taken as a beverage, it is really not germane to our discussion. We are quite prepared to concede that it may have been alcoholic wine. We simply do not know.

Our next text is…

And they gave him to drink wine mingled with myrrh: but he received it not. Mark 15:23

We have already commented on this text in examining the example of our Lord with respect to the use of alcoholic beverages. We note it here because it does fall under medicinal use, as that was the obvious intention of the Roman soldiers. The fact that Christ rejected it for the reasons previously noted does not change the fact that the application here was in a medical context. If ever there might have been a proper application of the principle of Proverbs 31:6 one might have thought that this would be it. Christ is about to die an excruciatingly painful death. To mitigate his suffering this drink is offered as an anaesthetic, or at least as an analgesic. The reasons for Christ refusing it were such that they do not necessarily apply to all persons. Therefore, this leaves open the possibility of others in similar circumstances accepting such relief. On the battlefields of the II World War it was common practice for the medics to administer morphine to wounded soldiers in great pain. It is still common for persons dying a painful death of terminal cancer to have their suffering alleviated by the use of morphine. However, morphine is derived from the opium poppy, as heroin is. The two substances are closely related. The latter is illegal and is proscribed, and its recreational use is both immoral and illegal. The former has widespread medicinal use. As with alcoholic wine, there is a significant moral difference between social and medicinal use.

Drink no longer water, but use a little wine for thy stomach's sake and thine often infirmities. 1 Timothy 5:23

The context of this text is again the medicinal use of wine. The question before us is "What kind of wine did Paul prescribe for Timothy?" Is Paul recommending fermented wine here or only the fresh blood of the grape? We don't know, and it really doesn't matter for our argument. Timothy would not ordinarily require apostolic permission to drink grape juice, so there is a strong possibility that Paul is recommending medicinal use of fermented wine. There is however one possibility that would indicate that he may have been recommending the use of grape juice. And that is if Timothy had undertaken to place himself under the vow of a Nazarite. This may seem unlikely in light of Paul's militant defense of the position that the Gentiles should not come under the ceremonial law. However, although Timothy was a Greek, he had a Jewish mother. For that reason Paul did circumcise him.

Then came he to Derbe and Lystra: and, behold, a certain disciple was there, named Timotheus, the son of a certain woman, which was a Jewess, and believed; but his father was a Greek: Which was well reported of by the brethren that were at Lystra and Iconium. Him would Paul have to go forth with him; and took and circumcised him because of the Jews which were in those quarters: for they knew all that his father was a Greek. Acts 16:1-3

Out of concern for opposition from the Jews, and because Paul considered Timothy at least partly Jewish, and because the ceremonial law was not immediately abolished, but was gradually phased out, Paul could go ahead and circumcise Timothy. Paul himself went into the temple and underwent ceremonial rituals of purification. He also took vows based on the ceremonial law. There was therefore a transitional period of time for the Jewish people as the ceremonial law was phased out and the New Covenant was implemented. And this allows for the possibility that Timothy took the vow of a Nazarite. If so that leaves us with another issue. If Timothy had actually made the vow of a Nazarite, could he be released from that vow by the Apostle, for reasons of health? I think so. Christ in his disputes with the Pharisees over the doctrine of the Sabbath, defended the eating of the showbread by David. Clearly Christ was teaching that matters of necessity, such as David's situation as he fled from Saul, justify overruling any merely ceremonial obligations. Timothy's sickness in the Apostle's eyes justified overruling normal prohibitions.

However, we still do not know for certain whether the prohibition that was being waived was a prohibition of alcoholic wine or a Nazarite vow that forbade wine of all sorts. Neither do we know what Timothy's stomach condition was, and what kind of wine the Apostle would have prescribed for it. Again, I am not a doctor. I know that many beneficial statements have been made for the medicinal value of grape juice. We also know that in the case of stomach ulcers alcohol is strictly forbidden on medical grounds. On the other hand it is also well established that in cases of nervous tension, where the stomach is all uptight, and digestion will not function normally, a small drink of alcoholic wine can settle the stomach and allow food to be taken. Its ability to provide some relief of tension and enable people to eat who are under severe stress is well documented. Ultimately, we simply do not know what kind of wine the Apostle recommended to Timothy, indeed, what kind of wine he commanded Timothy to take.

It really does not matter for our argument what kind of wine was involved here. If it was alcoholic wine, then we can note two things. One is that Timothy normally refused to take alcoholic wine. Secondly, abstinence from alcoholic wine may have been the norm in the Apostolic Church, and it took an injunction from an Apostle to get Timothy to partake of some. And if grape juice was prescribed then this text can not be used to ever justify the social use of alcoholic beverages. Either way our position remains essentially unchallenged by this text, and perhaps is even strengthened by it.

CHAPTER 9
OBJECTIONS

The four most common objections to the doctrine of temperance are:

1. Wine is wine. This is probably the most prevalent viewpoint. This is based upon the contemporary meaning of the word wine in the English language. This argument says that the Bible speaks approvingly of wine, and that means alcoholic wine, and that settles the issue for any Bible believer. This objection is based on the fallacy that the Bible was written in English. It takes our English Bible and elevates it to the status of the inerrant word of God. It forgets that it is only a fallible human translation of God's inerrant and inspired word, and is therefore subject to error. This view therefore ignores the effects and the consequences of the translation process. It presumes that the curse of the Tower of Babel, the confusion of languages, never occurred. Their Bible says that God approves of wine and that is the end of the argument.

This argument misses the key point, that the Scriptures were written in Hebrew and Greek, and that we need to examine the original languages and the words that the Holy Spirit chose to use to convey God's truth. It also ignores the fact that languages grow, develop, and change. Even the study of contemporary Greek and Hebrew, and the use of these words by modern Greeks and Israelis would not be final. And certainly the modern usage of the English word wine should not become the final arbiter in this debate. Not only is our culture and our society far removed from Biblical lands and their cultures, but it is also significantly different from the English society of 1611, when the Authorized Version of the Scriptures was first published.

The issue is that languages evolve. They change; they particularly change with respect to technology. It was during the generation of the 1950's and 60's that the automobile really came into its own. They developed a whole new set of words like V-8, stick shift, white walls, distributor, ignition, carburetor, convertible, etc., which either introduced new words into the language or gave a radically new meaning to existing words and phrases. The current generation is the computer generation. They have also significantly affected our language. They speak of hardware and software in an entirely new sense. They speak of RAM and ROM, of CD's and floppies, of hard drives and clock speeds, of microprocessors and modems. Our language will never be the same again. And what does all this mean? Well, it means for one thing, that we cannot be guided by the current definition of the word wine. There is considerable evidence that even some of the languages of Western Europe have traditionally used their word for wine in a generic sense. There is substantial historical evidence that the words for wine used by the nations of antiquity, as well as by the nations of Europe in recent centuries, have been used to refer to both the fermented and the unfermented juice of the grape, or of other fruits.*

It simply will not do to say that wine is wine. It is simply naive to assume that if the word wine is exclusively used to refer to fermented beverages today that it has always done so. And it is extremely myopic to assume that the translation in use has consistently and faithfully translated the original Scriptures without as much as an error or a misleading inference. It is only by thoroughly searching the

* William Patton in his book *Bible Wines or the Laws of Fermentation* discusses this in detail.

inspired text that we can hope to come, in some measure, to an accurate understanding of God's truth. And when we do that, the assumptions that favor the use of alcoholic wines evaporate.

2. Christ made wine, therefore it's use must be approved. This is of course, as the reader will logically recognize, a variation of the above objection. It again presumes that wine is wine and must be alcoholic. It compounds that misconception by assuming that Christ miraculously produced alcoholic wine for use at a wedding feast and concludes that therefore its approved use is established. However, wine is not necessarily wine in the sense that is being assumed. And as we have demonstrated, in the chapter on that subject, the wine produced at the wedding in Cana of necessity had to be non-alcoholic wine. The proper understanding of that miracle, and its context, is actually an argument against the use of alcoholic wine.

3. Christ drank wine, therefore its use must be approved. Again, as all these objections do, this one begs the question. It assumes that the wine that Christ drank is alcoholic and then concludes that it is approved. We have noted that Christ was scripturally forbidden to drink alcoholic wine. We have noted that the wine of which Christ partook at the Last Supper, by virtue of the law of the Passover, had to be non-alcoholic wine. We have noted that the Scriptures nowhere teach that Christ ever partook of alcoholic wine, that he explicitly rejected alcoholic wine when it was offered to him, and that the only wine that we know he did drink was non-alcoholic wine. The example of Christ, therefore, is against the use of alcoholic wine by his followers, rather than for it.

4. The condemnation of excess constitutes the approval of moderation. This is the fourth and final of the most common objections to the doctrine that the

Scriptures teach abstinence from alcoholic beverages. This argument states that since the Scriptures explicitly condemn "*much wine*" and "*excess of wine*," therefore by implication it approves of moderate use of wine, as it is the excess that is the object of the condemnation. This argument likes to quote Scriptures such as the following…

Likewise must the deacons be grave, not doubletongued, not given to much wine, not greedy of filthy lucre. 1 Timothy 3:8

The aged women likewise, that they be in behaviour as becometh holiness, not false accusers, not given to much wine, teachers of good things. Titus 2:3

For the time past of our life may suffice us to have wrought the will of the Gentiles, when we walked in lasciviousness, lusts, excess of wine, revellings, banquetings, and abominable idolatries. 1 Peter 4:3

However, it is a logical fallacy to assume that the condemnation of much, necessarily includes the approval of less. It is simply not true that when one condemns abuse and excess, that one is necessarily implying an approval of more moderate forms of what is being condemned. For instance, when one decries against those who speed excessively, and the dire consequences of that on our nation's highways, this does not imply that it is legitimate to speed, as long as one is only moderately over the limit. When a cry is made against an epidemic of vice, gambling, prostitution, drunkeness, etc., this does not imply that those who are offended will grant their moral approval of a little vice, of moderate levels of gambling, prostitution, and drunkeness. This entire argument is a logical fallacy. Let us examine a few Scriptures in this regard.

Be not over much wicked, neither be thou foolish: why shouldest thou die before thy time? Ecclesiastes 7:17

By much slothfulness the building decayeth; and through idleness of the hands the house droppeth through. Ecclesiastes 10:18

For when they speak great swelling words of vanity, they allure through the lusts of the flesh, through much wantonness, those that were clean escaped from them who live in error. 2 Peter 2:18

Now, does anyone really believe that when Solomon condemns much wickedness he is granting a license for a little wickedness? And when he decries the effects of much slothfulness is he really approving of moderate slothfulness? And similarly, when the Apostle Peter condemns much wantonness, is he teaching that Christians may display some wantonness as long as it does not reach the level of excess? Finally, examination of another text that is appealed to, in an attempt to sustain this objection, is very instructive, especially it in its context.

For the time past of our life may suffice us to have wrought the will of the Gentiles, when we walked in lasciviousness, lusts, excess of wine, revellings, banquetings, and abominable idolatries: Wherein they think it strange that ye run not with them to the same excess of riot, speaking evil of you. 1 Peter 4:3-4

Note that in the very next verse Peter condemns excess of riot. The word for "*riot*" (*asotia*), as we have noted earlier, means debauchery. Now this is one passage. The Apostle is uttering all this in virtually the same breath. If his condemnation of excess of wine implies approval of moderate use of wine, then his condemnation of excess of debauchery implies approval of moderate levels of debauchery. And who will believe that!

We have now reviewed the four leading objections against the doctrine of abstinence and have found them wanting. We can now proceed to other, if less well known, objections. There is actually only one other objection that I feel is worthy of note and of refutation. This is the argument raised by G. I. Williamson in his book *Wine in the Bible and the Church.* It somewhat pains me to have to debate with so eminent a servant of Jesus Christ as Rev. Williamson, who I hold in high esteem. However, I found at least one of the arguments in his book so fallacious and illogical, that I felt it required a response.

Now, initially, I want to say that Rev. Williamson makes a number of valid points. He is disputing with those who have made the traditional defense of abstinence. He is arguing against man-made rules of morality. He is arguing that we cannot add to the Scriptures. He is arguing that God alone is the Lord of the conscience. He is arguing that the Scriptures are our only rule of faith and practice. He is arguing that the law of God is sufficient for our instruction in righteousness. In short, he is taking issue with those who seek to maintain the doctrine of abstinence from alcoholic beverages without a proper scriptural foundation. He is taking issue with those who seek to compel the Lord's people to give up all use of alcoholic wine based on practical arguments against its abuse, etc. He is taking issue with those who ignore the plain statements of Scripture that appear to authorize the use of fermented wine. And in all that we agree with him. That many of the traditional defenses of temperance were deficient we acknowledged in our introduction. This book has been written to seek to provide a full and adequate scriptural basis for abstinence from alcohol. However, although I fully agree with Rev. Williamson's statements in this regard, I do not believe they apply as valid objections to this work.

There is, however, another class of statements made by Rev. Williamson that we want to take up. These statements taken together form another objection to the abstinence position. He argues from the following Scripture texts.

All things are lawful unto me, but all things are not expedient: all things are lawful for me, but I will not be brought under the power of any. 1 Corinthians 6:12

For every creature of God is good, and nothing to be refused, if it be received with thanksgiving: For it is sanctified by the word of God and prayer. 1 Timothy 4:4-5

Now the Spirit speaketh expressly, that in the latter times some shall depart from the faith, giving heed to seducing spirits, and doctrines of devils; Speaking lies in hypocrisy; having their conscience seared with a hot iron. Forbidding to marry, and commanding to abstain from meats, which God hath created to be received with thanksgiving of them which believe and know the truth. 1 Timothy 4:1-3

There is nothing from without a man, that entering into him can defile him: but the things which come out of him, those are they that defile the man. Mark 7:15

From these texts he argues that all things are lawful. He alleges that all material things are lawful, and that it is unscriptural to say that any material thing is in itself bad or evil. He states that every creature, that is all the material things that God has created, including fermented wine, is good and to be received with thanksgiving. He notes that commanding to abstain from meats, from specific foods, is a doctrine of devils. And finally, he notes that Christ taught that all sin and evil comes out of a man's heart and is not resident in some material thing. He states that to so teach is a form of Manichean dualism, the heresy that spirit is good but material things are bad. From all this he concludes that the doctrine of abstinence from alcoholic wine is a serious heresy.

Now, it is true that all moral evil comes from the hearts of God's creatures whether human or angelic. However, although physical inanimate things may not be evil in the moral sense, they can be evil in the sense of being very destructive, etc. In that sense the Bible calls floods, tempests, earthquakes, etc., evils that the Lord sends in judgment on the moral evil of his creation, that is, on sin. And in that sense we can be forbidden to partake of such foods, as their consumption could involve us in breaches of the sixth commandment.

The logical fallacy of this approach can be exposed by the fact that it proves too much. Taking purely natural things, we could then argue that a prohibition of marijuana and poisonous mushrooms would also be a doctrine of devils and a serious heresy! And if one denies the comparison is valid, one only needs to remember that on three occasions the Scriptures compare alcoholic wine to poison or venom. Moreover, fermented wine is not a natural creature of God as new wine is; it is a manufactured product, derived from a natural source. And so are heroin, cocaine, opium, etc., products that are manufactured from natural sources. Is the use of these substances for recreational use legitimate? Is the prohibition of these also a serious heresy? The fact is that the above noted class of substances are definitely prohibited. The book of Revelation in a number of texts explicitly condemns sorcery.

Neither repented they of their murders, nor of their ***sorceries****, nor of their fornication, nor of their thefts.* Revelation 9:21

And the light of a candle shall shine no more at all in thee; and the voice of the bridegroom and of the bride shall be heard no more at all in thee: for thy merchants were the great men of the earth; for by thy ***sorceries*** *were all nations deceived.* Revelation 18:23

But the fearful, and unbelieving, and the abominable, and murderers, and whoremongers, and ***sorcerers****, and idolaters, and all liars, shall have their part in the lake* *which burneth with fire and brimstone: which is the second death.* Revelation 21:8

For without are dogs, and ***sorcerers****, and whoremongers, and murderers, and idolaters, and whosoever loveth and maketh a lie.* Revelation 22:15

The word translated as sorceries is "*pharmakeia*" (φαρμακεία), from which we derive our modern words such as pharmacy and pharmaceuticals. In Greek it means drugs. Young defines it as meaning "enchantment with drugs." [Similarly, the word for sorcerer is "*pharmakeus*" (φαρμακεύς .)] Now, although comparisons between alcohol and hallucinatory drugs could be made, seeing they are both addictive, and both distort reality in the mind, that is not my point here. The point is that here are material substances whose use is condemned in the most explicit terms.

The whole principle of deducing from the texts cited by Rev. Williamson that no material substance can ever be prohibited is a logical fallacy that leads to absurdities. God himself has in the past and continues to prohibit specific foods. Before the great flood in the days of Noah God prescribed vegetarianism for the human race, prohibiting all other foods.

And God said, Behold, I have given you every herb bearing seed, which is upon the face of all the earth, and every tree, in the which is the fruit of a tree yielding seed; to you it shall be for meat. Genesis 1:29

And the LORD God planted a garden eastward in Eden; and there he put the man whom he had formed. And out of the ground made the LORD God to grow every tree that is pleasant to the sight, and good for food. Genesis 2:8-9

And the LORD God commanded the man, saying, Of every tree of the garden thou mayest freely eat. Genesis 2:16

Originally in the Garden of Eden, before the fall into sin, there was no death. Men ate only of the fruit of the ground. It was not until after the flood that God gave mankind permission to eat animal flesh.

Every moving thing that liveth shall be meat for you; even as the green herb have I given you all things. But flesh with the life thereof, which is the blood thereof, shall ye not eat. Genesis 9:3-4

However, even then, there remained a restriction on certain foods. Man was prohibited from eating blood. Animals had to be slaughtered and the blood drained. The blood could not be eaten. This prohibition of eating blood and of animals strangled, rather than properly slaughtered, remained in the New Testament Church. While the Gentiles were specifically exempted from the ceremonial law they remained under the dietary requirements that God gave to Noah after the flood.

Wherefore my sentence is, that we trouble not them, which from among the Gentiles are turned to God: But that we write unto them, that they abstain from pollutions of idols, and from fornication, and from things strangled, and from blood. Acts 5:19-20

And of course the ceremonial law itself contained extensive prohibitions of specific foods. Are we to conclude from Rev. Williamson's remarks that all this was wrong and that these restrictions, at least one of which remains with us until this day, constituted a doctrine of devils? This whole line of reasoning is fallacious. God can, and has in his word, prohibited certain natural foods at times in human history. God is sovereign. He has the right to do so. Our concern should not be to invent interpretations of Biblical texts to render such restrictions heretical, but to examine the Scriptures to see what restrictions God has placed us under in his moral law. That is what we have sought to do in this book and we have let God's word speak for itself. Again, we are left with the conclusion that there are no viable objections against the doctrine of abstinence from alcoholic beverages that can stand up to a careful scrutiny in the light of God's word.

CHAPTER 10
CONCLUSIONS

Originally, the scope of this book included two additional chapters. One was on the historic use of wine by Christians and devout Jews. It was thought that it might be an interesting historical study to examine what was the practice of the Jewish church and the early Christian church. The other chapter was to present the scientific argument. In that chapter the preservation of wine in Biblical times without it being subjected to fermentation was to be discussed. Though of obvious interest, I ultimately felt that such chapters were not necessary and might provoke questions and raise issues which would distract us from the scriptural argument that is the core of our case against alcoholic beverages.

In the final analysis these issues, though of interest, and perhaps helpful in rounding out the position, cannot determine the issue at hand. This book was written for Protestants. It was written for those who believe that the Bible is the only rule of faith and practice. It is for those who agree that God alone is Lord of the conscience and has left it free from the doctrines and commandments of men. Regardless of what was the practice of the early church, we cannot decide this issue by an appeal to tradition. It has been shown from the Scriptures, and I believe convincingly, that Christ, our great example, did not personally drink any alcoholic wine. It has been demonstrated that he did not provide any alcoholic wine at the wedding in Cana. And it has been shown that the wine used at the original Lord's Supper was also unfermented wine. That is all the history that we should need, for that is sacred history and its record is infallible, its statements are inerrant, and its testimony is authoritative. The sacred, inspired history has been allowed to speak, and we believe convincingly, against the use of alcoholic wine by the Lord's people.

There is however another scriptural clue as to the historical practice of the Apostolic Church found in the following text.

And they were all amazed, and were in doubt, saying one to another, What meaneth this? Others mocking said, These men are full of ***new wine****.* Acts 2:12-13

This is a fascinating text. It is the only text in the New Testament where the word for wine is not a translation of the Greek word "*oinos*." Rather the word used here is "*gleukos*" (γλεῦκος), which means sweet wine. Sweet wine is wine in which the sugar is still present and has not been fermented into alcohol. In fact, this is the word from which we derive the modern word "glucose," a certain type of sugar. Since it means sweet, or unfermented wine, the translators have rendered it as "*new wine*," the word "new" not being present in the Greek. Now, the context of this passage is the marvellous, miraculous events of the day of Pentecost. Many people were amazed at this dramatic outpouring of the Holy Spirit. Others mockingly scoffed and insinuated that these extraordinary happenings, including the speaking in tongues, were attributable to intoxication with wine. But interestingly these mockers didn't use the word "*oinos*," the word normally used to refer to fermented wine. They used a word that cannot mean fermented wine. Why? The only reason for this deduced by commentators is that they were being sarcastic. They knew that Christians did not drink alcoholic wine. They knew that Christians practiced abstinence from alcoholic beverages. So they mockingly insinuated that these drinkers of "*gleukos*" were drunk. They were scoffing that these people who pretended to be tee-totalers were drunk. It may be granted that this is based on an interpretation of this text, but it is hard to find a better one. And if it is true, then it is another historical argument that the Apostolic Church did not use alcoholic wine.

And like the historic argument, the scientific argument is neither necessary nor germane to our position. It is only briefly included because it might be helpful to the reader, and because it has been the basis for an objection to our position. The objection is that wine, since it was an ordinary article both of food and of commerce in ancient Middle Eastern societies, had to be commonly used in the fermented state, as they had no other way of preserving it. It is chiefly to blunt this objection that this issue is even being raised.

We acknowledge and admit that fermented wines were common in the typical societies of Biblical times. It is the thrust of the brief remarks we will now make on this subject to show that non-fermented wines were also common and constituted a normal part of both the food supply and the articles of commerce. This will add some support to the position that the words we have examined are in some instances generic words that stood for both types of wine. As for the ethical issues involved, these we leave entirely to be settled by the word of God.

Patten in his work "*Bible Wines*," deals extensively with this issue. Since he wrote in the nineteenth century, the science he quotes is somewhat dated, and according to my limited understanding, probably in error at times. He discusses the scientific requirements for the process of fermentation. These include not only the presence of sugar and yeast, but also the presence of air, that is, oxygen, the temperature ranges, and according to him the sugar concentration ranges at which wine can be fermented. We are not really concerned about the accuracy of his scientific claims. The chief value of this portion of his work is his extensive quotations from modern, and especially from ancient sources, about the fact and the methodology of preserving new wine, so as to inhibit and prevent fermentation. He clearly establishes the fact that the societies of Biblical times had the technology to preserve new wine, and that it was available and commonly used the year round. And, if this be the case, then the objection that it was only a seasonal food and that therefore the wine used was generally alcoholic fails. And, since he noted that these different types of wines were frequently referred to by the same word, it confirms our argument concerning the generic nature of some of these words.

However, ultimately our conclusions must rest on the word of God. In the past nine chapters our arguments have been strictly based on the Scriptures, on a "*thus saith the Lord,*" as the final arbiter of this issue that has for so long divided the Lord's people. As Isaiah said long ago to another generation, "*To the law and to the testimony: if they speak not according to this word, it is because there is no light in them*" (Isaiah 8:20). God's word has spoken. And when all the confusion and smoke has been cleared away, it has spoken clearly and convincingly against the social use of alcoholic beverages. When the foibles of specific translations, when our cultural prejudices, when the traditions of Christendom, have been set aside and God's word has been allowed to be the only rule of our faith, that is, our doctrine, and our practice, that is, how we live, then the results are not in question. If we submit to God's word, then we should come under conviction that its testimony is a coherent and sustained witness of warnings against alcoholic wine. The testimony of God's word is that the blessings that he pours out on his people never consist of alcohol, but of that new wine of which someday the Lord Jesus Christ will drink again, when he comes into his kingdom. Let us be faithful to his commands till that glorious day and look forward to that moment when we will drink it new with him in the Kingdom of God. **Amen.**

Scripture Index

Scripture Index (Con't)

About the American Presbyterian Press

The American Presbyterian Press was founded in 1979 by its Editor, Louis F. DeBoer, as the publishing ministry of the American Presbyterian Church. It republishes doctrinal and historical works of interest to Presbyterians in particular and to all Christians in general. It also publishes contemporary works that are thought to be of benefit to the Lord's people, especially those of the Reformed faith, as well as particular works that teach and expound the distinctive doctrines of the American Presbyterian Church.

It has published the following works which are still in print at the time of this writing.

Charles Hodge: A Constitutional History of the Presbyterian Church in the USA.
Thomas M'Crie: The Life of Melville
E. C. Wines: The Hebrew Republic
Edmund B. Fairfield: Letters On Baptism
W. A. MacKay: Immersion and Immersionists
L. F. DeBoer: The New Phariseeism
L. F. DeBoer: The Divine Covenants
L. F. DeBoer: Lord of the Conscience

The American Presbyterian Press also offers a full line of evangelistic tracts, customized with your church information. These can be reviewed on its website, which also offers articles, commentary, book reviews, etc. It also has a number of forthcoming titles. To see what is currently in print, what is forthcoming, to read reviews of these works and to obtain price and ordering information visit us online at **www.amprpress.com** or write us at…

1459 Boston Neck Road, Saunderstown, RI 02874